ENDORSEMENTS

"The world got a little bit brighter after reading *Nothing Is Wasted*. Thank you, Joseph Bentz, for plugging a missing hole in contemporary Christian teaching—balance in tragedy, and finding hope without glossing over difficulty."

Pastor Jake McCandless
Mount Vernon Baptist Church
Mount Vernon, Arkansas

"This invaluable book is for anyone who has ever questioned why life is so painful, chaotic, and messy. Joseph Bentz powerfully unveils God's continuous thread of redemption that is woven throughout the complicated and broken tapestry of our frayed world."

Pastor Ed Simons
South Central Ohio District
Church of the Nazarene

NOTHING
How God Redeems What Is Broken
IS WASTED

Joseph Bentz

BEACON HILL PRESS
OF KANSAS CITY

Copyright © 2016 by Joseph Bentz
Beacon Hill Press of Kansas City
PO Box 419527
Kansas City, MO 64141
beaconhillbooks.com

978-0-8341-3551-2

Cover Design: Jeff Gifford
Interior Design: Sharon Page

Library of Congress Cataloging-in-Publication Data

Names: Bentz, Joseph, 1961- author.
Title: Nothing is wasted : how God redeems what is broken / Joseph Bentz.
Description: Kansas City, Missouri : Beacon Hill Press of Kansas City, 2016.
  | Includes bibliographical references.
Identifiers: LCCN 2015042233 | ISBN 9780834135512 (pbk.)
Subjects: LCSH: Redemption--Christianity. | Suffering--Religious aspects—Christi-
anity. | Consolation. | Providence and government of God—Christianity.
Classification: LCC BT775 .B385 2016 | DDC 248.8/6--dc23 LC record available at
http://lccn.loc.gov/2015042233

All Scripture quotations, unless indicated, are taken from The *Holy Bible:*
New International Version® (NIV®). Copyright © 1973, 1978, 1984, 2011 by
Biblica, Inc.™ Used by permission of Zondervan. All rights reserved world-
wide. www.zondervan.com.

The internet addresses, email addresses, and phone numbers in this book
are accurate at the time of publication. They are provided as a resource. Beacon Hill Press of Kansas City does not endorse them or vouch for their content or permanence.

10 9 8 7 6 5 4 3 2 1

TABLE OF CONTENTS

1 ❧ THE SONG OF REDEMPTION

When you glance around the world, you may not think you see much redemption. You may notice more trouble instead. Terrorists blow up innocent children. Bombs demolish homes and send frightened citizens fleeing toward the squalor of refugee camps. Disease sweeps through impoverished nations and wipes out hundreds, their bodies tossed aside. Drought kills crops and puts farmers out of business. Politicians posture, blame, and take feckless stabs at solving intractable problems. Celebrities enmesh themselves in scandals, providing the public a perverse escape from all the real tragedy of the world.

Closer to home, maybe your own life isn't faring so well either. You're worried about money. You fret about work. What about the crises in your family? What about all the sickness among the people you love? Where is your life headed? Even if your life is going well now, you wonder how long it can last. All around you, everything is falling apart. People you love are getting older. *You* are getting older, much faster than you'd like. The possibility of disaster lurks in every automobile trip, every medical checkup, every unknown terrorist's scheme.

If you let yourself dwell on it, you realize nothing is as stable as it looks. Temporariness and decay are built into everything around you. The building in which you stand looks solid, but you know it is slowly crumbling. The car you drive will be obsolete in a matter of years. No matter how trendy you try to be, your clothes are beginning to go out of style from the moment you put them on. When you look at photos of yourself in them twenty years from now, assuming you live that long, you may even be embarrassed that you wore them. Your haircut, the music you listen to, the way you decorate your home, will all become hopelessly old-fashioned faster than you think. You yourself will fade and then die.

One way to look at life is as a series of losses. We lose loved ones, our youth, our decaying possessions, and eventually our lives. The world is a fallen, suffering, fading place. In that kind of world, how are we supposed to see hints of redemption?

The pattern of loss is pervasive. The fallen, corrupt nature of the world is real. But there is also a countervailing force at work in the world. In the midst of all this loss beats a relentless pulse of redeeming love and good that thrusts itself through the chaos and pain. It does not obliterate the pain, but it does not allow it to be wasted either. Good is wrenched from pain, like a gold nugget pried from deep underground.

Learning to Hear Redemption's Song

When you watch a movie, it may have a theme song that is played in fragments of various lengths throughout the film. The music may be slowed down or sped up a little to fit the action on screen, and at times the few snippets of song may be so brief and subtle that you're not consciously aware of them. But the effect is powerful anyway. Whenever you hear about that movie for days or weeks afterward, you may still remember pieces of that melody.

That's what redemption is like. God has blended it into the world. It's as if God is saying, *This song is so good, and it so embodies what I'm all about, that I'm going to spread traces of it throughout the movie.* Sometimes it will be loud and obvious; other times, you'll barely be able to recognize it's the same song. By the time the show is over, you'll know it. You'll be humming it all day.

In this book, I want to play the song of redemption. I want you to hear it in all its variations, in places where you can't miss it and in places where you would least expect it.

It's easy to find hints of redemption in beautiful elements of life, obviously, in things that make you glad you're alive even when the rest of the world stinks. Loving relationships, the joy of meaningful work, the deep pleasures of music, walks on sandy beaches, hikes through forests, good meals, enjoyable books, and countless other good facets of life certainly offset many of life's harsher realities. These redeeming elements of life are easy to see.

Does God also plant redemption in ugly, smelly, unpleasant things? Can it be found in things people see only as destructive, or mean, or sad? Can redemption spring from things that people believe have no value? Can even the worst circumstances life has to offer give rise to redemption?

When a Destructive Insect Embodies Redemption

The boll weevil is an ugly little insect that loves cotton. Over the past hundred years, it has caused billions of dollars in damage to cotton crops in the United States and elsewhere. Numerous farmers across the decades have gone bankrupt because of this one pest. Scientists have used every means they can think of to try to eradicate it—pesticides, wasps, fungi, specially engineered anti-weevil cotton plants, and other methods. The fight against it continues to this day, and the eradication programs have been largely successful.

No one sheds a tear for the boll weevil. Just about everybody wants to kill it. So I was surprised when my friend Jim Davis, who lives in Alabama, a state that historically has been plagued with weevils, told me that a town named Enterprise, Alabama, has a boll weevil monument prominently displayed in the center of its downtown.

A monument to a destructive insect would be surprising in any town, but for Enterprise, Alabama, to honor such a creature seems especially strange, considering the destruction the boll weevil has wreaked on that town and the surrounding county. As the town's historians report, in the early twentieth century, the boll weevil destroyed almost 60 percent of the county's main crop of cotton, and farmers were at risk of utter ruin.[1] Their failure would have meant devastation for the entire economy of that region.

The monument the town built to this pest in 1919 features a statue of a woman standing in Statue-of-Liberty-like robes, her arms held high above her head. In her hands, on top of a kind of pedestal, stands a large and ugly boll weevil. A flowing fountain surrounds this statue.

Is it a joke?

The farmers in Coffee County, Alabama, where Enterprise is located, were determined not to let the boll weevil defeat them. Instead, they turned its destructive behavior into an opportunity to diversify their crops and be more successful in the long run. If the crisis of the boll weevil had not forced the issue, they might never have made changes and would have missed out on the prosperity the shift brought them. Peanuts in particular became an especially profitable crop for the region. As the Enterprise history relates, "By 1917, Coffee County produced and harvested more peanuts than any other county in the nation. (In 1993, Coffee County ranked 4th in the state of Alabama with 128,000 acres planted in peanuts.)"[2] The plaque that accompanies the monument states, "In profound appreciation of the Boll Weevil and what it has done as the herald of Prosperity this monument was erected by the citizens of Enterprise, Coffee County, Alabama." The work of a pest was redeemed.

Smelly Carcass or Tasty Feast?

Although a monument to a bug is unusual, redemptive elements scattered throughout the uglier side of nature are common. For instance, it's hard to think of many things uglier than a carcass, but in nature, such a thing is not wasted. Whales, for example, can weigh eighty tons or more, and when dead ones wash up on a beach, as they do occasionally, they are smelly, rotting, and hard to dispose of. But in the ocean, where they belong, one dead whale becomes a *meal* that can feed countless other animals for *decades*.

When a whale carcass sinks to the seafloor, the first animals that feast on it are interested in removing the flesh from the bones. Hagfish, rattails, crabs, sharks, and other scavengers pick the bones clean. But the meal has not even started for a whole variety of other creatures that enjoy dining on the bones.

Scientists at the Monterey Bay Aquarium Research Institute (MBARI) wanted to learn more about the bone-eating animals, so they dragged five dead whales off the beach and sank them with weights at various depths in the ocean to see what they could find out. As they kept track of what came to dine on these tasty carcasses, they discovered fifteen new species of bone-eating worms and several new species of bone-eating snails.[3]

With all these creatures chomping at flesh and bones, the MBARI scientists estimate their five whale carcasses will be gone within about ten years, but in other areas, where different carcasses are deeper, the food source may last from fifty to a hundred years. As the carcasses continue to disappear, the researchers keep finding even more new species of limpets, worms, amphipods, and snails.[4] From the whale's perspective, of course, its own death may seem a disaster, but for many other hungry creatures, life springs from that death.

What About My Own Pain? How Could It Be Anything but Wasted Suffering?

It's one thing to spot hints of redemption in things like whale carcasses and boll weevils, but how much will those hints mean to people if they can't find similar clues of redemption in their own difficult lives?

What about people who suffer the worst things life has to offer? For example, what about someone whose young child is killed? What about someone whose own health is wrecked by accident or cancer or other illness? What about people whose dreams for their future are shattered by circumstances beyond their control? Is that pain wasted? Is pain the final word in the lives of those people, or is there something more?

I asked them. I went to people who suffered those catastrophes and asked them whether they saw any hints of redemption in the midst of their suffering. Rather than interpret their experiences on my own, I wanted to know how *they* perceived what had happened to them. For most of them, the pain still continues, but they also find threads of redemption in their own stories. They do so not in a way that brushes aside or minimizes their suffering but in ways that acknowledge that something else is going on. Suffering is at work in their lives, but so are other forces.

What Meaning Can Be Salvaged from the Mess?

This book does not treat suffering lightly, nor does it try to explain it away or find an explanation for why it exists in the first place. The world is filled with many horrors. People do cruel things, and people are victims of tremendous evil. It is an off-kilter world, damaged by sin. If that were not so, there would be no need for redemption. As a Christian, I believe that if the world were not a fallen place, Jesus Christ would not have had to come and be crucified to save it.

To revise an image from G.K. Chesterton, think of the world as a beautiful ship that has been wrecked on the rocks of sin. We survived and have found ourselves beached on an island, with some of the ship's possessions having washed ashore with us. We await an ultimate rescue, but in the meantime, we make the best of those salvaged pieces we have pulled from the wreck. Should we see our state as good or bad? On one hand, we survived the wreck! We are saved. On the other hand, we are not yet rescued and at home. We do not have all the possessions from the original ship, but perhaps the real surprise is that we have *anything*, given the fact that the ship went down.

God could have walked away from the sinful world. He could have destroyed it and started again from scratch, but he loved us too much to do so. Instead, through Jesus Christ, God held out the promise of something eternally good being pulled from the muck of the sin-damaged world. The story of that divine reversal is told most fully in the Bible. *Echoes* of that story can be heard in thousands of other stories—in movies, novels, children's stories, and elsewhere. Hints of it pervade our popular entertainment and literature, even when people aren't intentionally telling it. What is that central story of redemption?

If you simply read the Bible straight through in order to find it, you may succeed, but you would almost certainly feel overwhelmed at many points along the way. The story of redemption in Scripture does not follow the tidy story structure you may have learned in a high school literature class, with a beginning, rising action, climax, falling action, and resolution. Nor does it follow the neat, three-act structure of a screenplay. It's messy.

I remember how bothered I was as a young Christian when I first read the Bible all the way through. It seemed so complicated and went off in so many directions. There were all those generations of chaos, bad behavior, and disobedience, with an occasional breakthrough in which God freed the Israelites from Pharaoh or helped his people win a battle. I would read about a few good kings here and there, but then there were more outrageous acts of disobedience by their sons who followed them. That would be followed by books of prophecies of doom, with a little bit of hope sprinkled in.

I read all that even before I got to the books about Jesus. The four Gospels offered the uplifting accounts of Jesus's teaching and miracles, of course, but they were also filled with people resisting him, not understanding him, and finally crucifying him. The rest of the Bible was similarly untidy, with all those letters focused on straightening out troubled churches and talking of imprisonments and persecutions and other difficulties. Then the whole book ended with one of the most difficult sections of all—Revelation. That book held out the promise of eternity with the resurrected Christ in a new heaven and a new earth but did so in the midst of head-spinning imagery that challenged my young mind.

Why, I wondered, *didn't God clean this up and put it in a neater package?*

Other writers, theologians, and preachers *have* told the gospel story more simply, and it has been very helpful for them to do so. I first learned about the Christian faith as a child from teachers and preachers who told the story in ways I could understand. As I got older, I relied on others to help me grasp it even better at whatever level of understanding I found myself. I am still doing that today, finding new writers and teachers who capture the essence of the story of God's redemption.

When I was a college student, for example, I was particularly moved by C.S. Lewis's *Mere Christianity*. I came across his book at a time when I was hungry for a deeper understanding of the faith that had gripped me so strongly as a child and teenager. I had encountered Christ and had become a passionate follower, but there was still so much I didn't understand. I found Lewis's book challenging, but I also felt liberated by the way he cut through the web of theological side issues and speculation to get to the essence of the Christian faith, which he states this way:

> We are told that Christ was killed for us, that His death has washed out our sins, and that by dying He disabled death itself. That is the formula. That is what has to be believed. Any theories we build up as to how Christ's death did all this are, in my view, quite secondary: mere plans or diagrams to be left alone if they do not help us, and, even if they do help us, not to be confused with the thing itself.[5]

I was thrilled to read that statement because, even though I had questions about all kinds of Christian issues, I didn't want to miss "the thing itself" when it came to redemption in Christ. That "thing itself"—salvation through Jesus Christ and the promise of eternity with him—is the plot of the Bible's story; but, in Scripture as in life, redemption shows up not only in the main plot but also in the strange little subplots.

Nothing Is Wasted will trace this redemptive pattern in some of those unexpected corners of life—in the work of the dung beetle, in the goo of a chrysalis, in the blasting of a woman's career dreams, in a car accident that leaves a woman broken and bleeding on the road. At first glance some of these examples will look like sheer ugliness. It will seem impossible that any good could come from them. But that's how redemption works. It grows up from smelly, sometimes disgusting, soil.

The sprawling nature of the story of redemption—the way God has scattered and buried hints of it throughout every area of life—is perhaps one reason why Scripture itself looks so fragmented and varied. The subplots play out in psalms, parables, history, prophecies, and poetry. People fail God time and time again throughout the book, but instead of giving up on them, instead of stopping the story right there and starting over with someone else, God uses the flawed people and complicated situations to keep the central story of redemption moving forward.

Take Abraham and Sarah. They are two of the greatest people in Scripture, but their lives are full of complications. When God is slow about fulfilling his promise to provide them a son, Sarah comes up with a plan for Abraham to have the child through her servant, Hagar. Ishmael is born through that arrangement, but his birth leads to family strife, abuse, and endless future difficulties in the years to come.

Is God's plan thrown hopelessly off course? No. Isaac is born to Abraham and Sarah, and the promise is fulfilled. Hagar keeps going too, running away for a time but then moving back in with Abraham and Sarah and making the best of her life. The angel of the Lord promises Hagar, "I will increase your descendants so much that they will be too numerous to count," but he also says of Ishmael, "He will be a wild donkey of a man; his hand will be against everyone and everyone's hand against him, and he will live in hostility toward all his brothers" (Genesis 16:10, 12).

Trouble and promise live side by side in this story. It's messy, but God's thread of redemption is woven through it.

Even in the stories of the Bible that look disturbing or just plain strange to modern readers, redemption still emerges from the mess. In one of my literature courses, I teach the story of Lot's wife, found in Genesis 19. As Sodom and Gomorrah are about to be destroyed, Lot and his family flee the scene. They are told not to look back, but Lot's wife disobeys, looks back, and is turned into a pillar of salt. No other information about her is given. Many modern poets have written about Lot's wife in order to speculate on facts and motives the Bible leaves out, such as: Why does she turn around? What is going on in her mind? Rebellion? Longing? Suicide? Modern writers and biblical commentators have endlessly debated and retold the story. But there is another strange episode in the aftermath of this story that bothers my students even more than Lot's wife's sad demise.

According to Genesis 19, Lot's two daughters survive the destruction of Sodom and Gomorrah and move with Lot to the mountains of Zoar. Since there is a shortage of men there, the daughters decide to get their father drunk and have sex with him so they can preserve the family line. They both get pregnant and give birth to sons.

My students squirm when they read this story. What are we to think of it? Why on earth is a story like this even in the Bible, of all places? The passage tells only the facts and gives no direction to the reader on what to think about this story. Are we supposed to see what happens as evil? Twisted? Or is it somehow hopeful, a story of survivors who do what they have to do?

Commentators are divided about what it means. Some see the episode as a kind of punishment for Lot for offering up his daughters for sexual purposes earlier in the story. He offered them for abuse, and now he is the one abused.

Other commentators, however, find redemption even in this troublesome episode. Lot's firstborn daughter gives birth to a boy she names Moab, and the reader is told that he is the father of the Moabites to this day. Ruth, for whom a book of the Bible is named, is a Moabite, a descendant of that child born under such strange circumstances. Ruth is also one of the few women named in the genealogy of Jesus, in the book of Matthew.

So, from this disturbing episode, which seems such a sad aftermath of Lot's rescue from the destruction of Sodom and Gomorrah, redemption springs, even though it takes hundreds of years to happen.

We could fill pages with stories like this from both the Old Testament and New Testament. Look at episodes from the lives of Moses, David, Hannah, Jeremiah, Gideon, Joshua, and many others. In the New Testament, Paul is repeatedly imprisoned, but, rather than stopping or slowing down the spread of the gospel, those setbacks actually speed it up as he spreads the message in Rome and elsewhere and writes his letters that still lead people to Christ today.

The messiness of the Bible represents God's willingness to enter into even the most hopeless of circumstances and draw something good out of them. The Bible does not follow a predictable narrative, and neither does my own life. In both Scripture and my life, I see God's persistent thread of redemption, and that gives me hope.

What Difference Does It Make?

If you begin to see the hints of redemption scattered throughout the world, what difference does that make? Why should you bother with it?

I have known people who impoverish their lives by having too narrow a definition of redemption. Some Christians believe in ultimate redemption in Jesus Christ, but they miss the thousands of other places throughout their lives where God has lovingly planted reminders of redemption. Faced with catastrophe in their own lives, they see only the loss, and they either reject or else fail to see the good that may also spring from it. They miss it in nature, in music, in the portions of life considered ugly or useless, in the stories that bombard them throughout the day. Without realizing they are doing so, they have relegated God to a particular, crucial—but narrow—sliver of life, and refuse to open their eyes to his presence in the rest of the world.

I know other people who do the opposite. They acknowledge the redemptive thread in the ways that new life might burst from the devastation of a forest fire, or how a caterpillar is transformed into a butterfly, but they wouldn't think to tie that to God's larger plan of redemption for human beings and for creation itself. They either don't believe in this ultimate redemption through Jesus Christ, or, if they do, they see spiritual redemption as a separate category from everything else.

People have always missed the clues of redemption, not only in our day—when open skepticism is more common—but even when people had Jesus right there in front of them. Take the story of the man born blind in John 9. Jesus and his disciples see him as they are walking down the road on the Sabbath. The disciples, instead of seeing this encounter as an opportunity for Jesus to turn this man's life around through a miraculous healing, instead want to turn it into a theological debate. Whose sin caused the blindness, they ask, the blind man's or his parents'? Neither, Jesus says. Instead, this encounter is "so that the work of God might be displayed in him" (John 9:3). And Jesus heals him.

You might expect that everyone would be happy about this—a man who has been blind his whole life now can see! Instead, controversy erupts, and the beauty of the miracle itself almost gets forgotten. The religious authorities launch an investigation. Jesus has performed this healing on the Sabbath, so it's a technical violation. The newly sighted man gets hauled in for questioning. So do his parents. The parents wither under the questioning of these powerful men. They decline to answer questions. They throw it back to the son: "Ask him. He is of age; he will speak for himself" (John 9:21).

Everyone is running scared and missing the miracle, but the man who is no longer blind refuses to call Jesus a sinner, as the authorities want him to. He knows the good thing Jesus has done for him and won't deny it. "Whether he is a sinner or not, I don't know," he says. "One thing I do know. I was blind but now I see!" (John 9:25).

The man has learned not only to see physically but also to see in the sense of understanding. He sees, and he *sees*. That's the kind of sight I want. His story shows what different people choose to do with God's hints of redemption. Some deny them. Some ignore them. Some welcome them and thank God for them.

I want to learn to decipher the hints better. I want to learn to see the ways that God wrests something good from even the most terrible things of life. If you want that too, then I invite you to read on.

Go to beaconhillbooks.com/go/nothingiswasted for a free downloadable study guide that includes questions for deeper personal reflection as well as activities for use in a small group setting.

2 ⨠ REDEMPTION IN TRAGIC CIRCUMSTANCES

How would you answer the question: *What's the worst thing that could happen?*

What circumstance sounds so horrible to you that you can barely allow your imagination to touch it?

For parents, the worst thing may be the death of a child. For some, the diagnosis of cancer fills them with dread. For young married couples, the premature loss of a spouse could top the list. For still others, a life-altering accident might be what they fear most.

Imagine that one of these things happens to you. How might that event change your outlook on the idea that God has scattered redemption throughout the universe, and that even in a fallen world, nothing is wasted?

Now imagine something further. What if two of these horrible, life-changing events happened to you at the same time? Would you still be likely to believe in redemption?

What if your situation were even worse? Let's imagine you're a married man with five children. Your sixteen-year-old daughter dies in an accident. The following year, your first granddaughter dies at birth, and not too long after that, your brother's wife dies of cancer. Several years later, your twin teenage sons are in an accident that paralyzes one from the waist down and inflicts a life-threatening cervical injury on the other. In the same year, your mother dies, another son undergoes an emergency appendectomy, and just when you think things can't possibly get worse, you are diagnosed with prostate cancer.

Would it be possible for you to ever believe again that redemption is at the core of God's purposes?

The scenario I just described is real, and I know the man who suffered all these catastrophes. His name is Jerry Deans, and I met him where I have met many people who have endured some of life's worst disasters—at a writers conference. I have taught at many conferences, helping writers get their books into publishable shape. Over the years I have seen that many people write out of pain. Like all of us, they hope for good times in their daily lives, but their books rarely spring from the easy times. Instead, pain is what they feel compelled to discuss. However, over and over, I have seen that pain is almost never the final word. Redemption is almost always at the heart of these stories. The writers work through their own catastrophes and feel compelled to offer hope to others.

When I heard Jerry's story, with its long string of devastating circumstances, I wondered how he could possibly be anything but bewildered, angry, or bitter. Yet, if the redemptive idea that nothing is wasted has any validity, then it can be true only if it works in the midst of life's worst circumstances.

After that conference, I couldn't get Jerry's story out of my mind. I kept in touch with him, and as I began to write this book, I looked back at what he wrote and confronted him with new questions of my own. I also got in touch with other people whose stories of disaster have moved me. As I approached them with my questions and asked permission to write about their stories, I was determined to see what conclusions *they* drew about what had happened to them rather than trying to find redemption in their stories myself. Did *they* believe their tragedies served no purpose? Did they blame God? Did they feel bitter toward God? Did good emerge from their horrible circumstances that could have come in no other way?

I know tragedy does push some people toward bitterness and hopelessness. Even people who have faced only a fraction of the cruel circumstances that Jerry Deans endured can be ruined for life. So why didn't that happen to Jerry and the others whose stories I heard?

I was repeatedly surprised as I listened to how people who had faced some of life's worst blows processed their own stories. I also read published memoirs and magazine articles in which people reflected on the meaning of the suffering they had experienced. No circumstance seemed beyond redemption—death, illness, bankruptcy, career meltdowns, accidents, personal failures.

Most people I encountered don't learn much from tragedy *while* they're experiencing it. They're too busy fending off pain. For most of the people I talked to or whose stories I read, the gift of seeing anything good arise from their circumstances did not come quickly or easily. Only when they looked back from a considerable distance could they see the ways in which the pain had served some purpose. Here are some of the things I learned from them.

Tragedy strips away the illusion of self-sufficiency and makes people aware of their utter dependence on God.

Until the death of their beloved teenage daughter Shantel, Jerry and his wife had felt protected by what he calls a "ring of fire," an image that came from a pastor who brought Jerry and his wife into church membership with this prayer: "Lord, surround this family with a ring of fire and protection from anything that might come against them." The family had moved to a new town, where Jerry found success in his dream job, and his wife and children thrived.

Then came the day of the accident. Shantel, who was an excellent swimmer, went to a nearby lake at a state park for a routine afternoon of fun. When she went missing, Jerry and his wife refused to believe her drowning was a possibility. It didn't make sense, given her skills and strength. They went to the lake and waited and prayed. Police investigated. Divers searched. Then came the worst moment.

Jerry heard divers ask for a body bag, and the truth of what had happened sank in. The ring of fire had been abruptly extinguished.

Jerry said, "It is difficult to describe the devastation that comes with such a sudden and unnatural loss. It crashes into and crushes your life in every way imaginable; physically, emotionally, spiritually. Losing Shantel took us into uncharted depths of sadness and depression we had never before experienced." He and his wife struggled not only with overwhelming grief but also with the shock that the protection they had once felt had now been stripped away. If their daughter could be taken away from them so suddenly, then what else might happen?

The events that followed only confirmed their sense that any protection they might have once imagined had only been an illusion. A year after Shantel's death, their daughter Tiffany carried their first grandchild to full term then lost her at birth. After that, Jerry's brother's wife died from brain cancer. Jerry and Patsi struggled not only to figure out the meaning of all these tragedies but also simply how to bear them. And, though they could not know it, their long string of disasters was far from over. "The bubble of invulnerability most of us live in had burst," said Jerry, "and there was no way to put it back in place."

If the ring of fire was an illusion, and God did not operate the way Jerry thought he did, where would that leave Jerry's faith?

What was reality? What would replace Jerry's old assumptions about God? In Jerry's case, his spiritual disruption ultimately led to a deeper and more authentic relationship with God, but that outcome was not a foregone conclusion by any means.

For anyone, this kind of spiritual shipwreck is a season of great risk. Some turn away from God altogether when their assumptions about God are overturned. The catastrophes Jerry experienced led him to confront the deepest spiritual questions. There is risk in such confrontation, but there is also risk in *not* confronting them, in floating through life with an easy theology that denies harsh realities and avoids the toughest questions.

Disaster can serve as a spiritual wake-up call in many ways. I was moved by the story of Kathleen Anderson, who wrote in *Christianity Today* of the impact that debilitating health problems have had on her spiritual life. In earlier days she was a powerlifter and also a runner who completed marathons and ran nearly seven hundred miles during her senior year of high school on the track team. She worked hard to make the best of her athletic abilities and took pride in her unusual strength. Then she was struck with numerous physical setbacks. "Now," she writes, "after four major surgeries and myriad health issues, I can raise my left arm with difficulty, have many allergies, and frequently face nausea, sinus problems, fitful sleep, and fatigue. When I tell my students that I used to be a powerlifter, they glance at my skinny arms in disbelief."[1]

What could such a radical change in lifestyle possibly produce besides resentment and disappointment? In fact, Anderson has struggled with such feelings: "Bodily dysfunctions have denied me my fierce independence and protectiveness of my privacy; I am the vulnerable, exposed slab on the table, ready for the surgeon's carving knife. It's a shattering thing to look one's mortality in the face." And yet, she believes her pain has not been wasted. She says that, "in stripping me of the illusion of self-reliance, these ailments have also increased my gratitude for God's presence in the goodness of those who have aided me."[2]

Anderson does not deny how much she hates the ailments that have afflicted her, but she also sees that her path has been strewn with unexpected benefits. God has sent her "mysterious comforts," such as a time when she was about to enter into surgery and dreaded being alone. In a pre-op waiting room, where no one else was supposed to be, a kind old man sat and talked to her. The nurse tried to kick him out, but he stayed anyway, insisting he had permission to be there. His presence comforted Anderson when she needed it most.

Just as she has treasured the caring presence of others during her ordeals, she believes her suffering has increased her empathy for others. It has also made her more acutely aware of God's presence. "The fragility of my bodily house serves as a reminder of the glory of our permanent house with God," she says. "He is present with us in our pain and in the silence and loneliness that come with it."[3]

Beautiful redemptions. Still, as I hear the stories of tragedy and affliction, I can't help but picture people like Jerry Deans and Kathleen Anderson at the lowest points of their distress, and I wonder, are the spiritual awakenings that spring from such tragedy enough? As Jerry mourns his sixteen-year-old daughter on some lonely night, or as Kathleen endures the frustrations of yet another health issue, is it enough for them to know that they see reality more clearly, and that illusions have been stripped away? Would it be preferable to live in illusions, in blind contentment, if that meant avoiding the pain?

No one *chooses* the circumstances these people have endured. Few, if any, of us *ask* for our illusions to be stripped away at any cost. Most of us, if we were actually given the choice, would almost certainly say the cost is too high. A change of perspective or other redemptive change in us, no matter how liberating it may be in the long run, is a tough sell *now*, when we're suffering. When we're focused on *now*, and a beloved family member is dead or our bodies are betraying us, it's hard to give much thought to anything but the pain.

The tragedies come unasked for, but what if they never came? In the corrupt world in which we live, who knows what kind of people any of us would turn out to be without the harsh, spiritual wake-up calls that sometimes interrupt our lives? What if we got everything we wanted? Given the selfish bent of human nature, would we become arrogant? Materialistic? Self-absorbed? Entitled? Dismissive of the needs of others? Those are common enough traits even *with* the reminders of how fleeting and fragile life is. Harsh circumstances may, if we don't let them be wasted, at least lead us to ask: *What does it all mean? Where am I headed after this life? What is reality?*

The redemptions, like the suffering, emerge without anyone choosing them. But people do have a choice about their response. No one has to accept the redemptive elements of a tragedy. They can be rejected or denied. People are free to emerge from tragic circumstances just as spiritually blind as when they entered into them. Kathleen, Jerry, and others whose stories I have gathered chose to accept the good that came from their circumstances, while not denying the bad. They did not perceive that God pushed them into suffering to teach them a lesson. Instead, they describe sensing God's presence *in the midst* of their suffering—at least eventually—and they particularly sensed God in the people who helped them through the tough times. God moved close to them, and they chose to embrace him.

Even when redemption begins to emerge from tragedy, it may only be later that a person recognizes the good that God has brought out of disaster.

"You must die a series of deaths and be born again into a new life God has prepared for you." When Jerry Deans looks back on the series of catastrophes that plagued his life and the spiritual growth that emerged from it, this concise statement is how he now encapsulates an important element of what he learned. Moving into that new life was not easy, and the changes that happened to him did not come in any predictable way. One day during his ordeal, for example, Jerry visited the Vietnam War Memorial in Washington, DC, and pondered the names of the thousands of dead soldiers that fill the wall. As he calculated how many thousands of grieving families those names represent, important questions came to his mind: *Why* not *you, Jerry? What makes you so special that you would somehow be beyond the reach of the bad things that happen to the people in this world?* If so many others have been forced to deal with sudden death, how could he expect to be spared from the same kind of loss?

The grief Jerry and his wife experienced made them feel the need for support from others who had suffered such loss. They contacted their pastor, who gathered other parents who had lost children. A support group formed that turned into a lifeline for Jerry and Patsi. At first, the meetings were difficult and exhausting, filled with crying and tangible pain. Jerry wondered whether the experience hurt more than helped. But he and Patsi finally felt they were with people who understood. Jerry said, "We no longer felt the loneliness and isolation. As we discovered that others had experienced the same feelings and reactions, ours lost much of their sting. We came to realize we were on a journey that none of us would have chosen. But we were not alone on that journey; we had traveling companions who were willing to encourage us and show us the way."

These insights and others like them were the *beginning* of a process God was leading Jerry through, not the end. He says, "We began to sense that we were on a journey of recovery and that a loving, compassionate presence was guiding us. The pain of our loss continued long after we expected it to be over. But gradually we stopped asking God, 'Why?' and started asking, 'What now, Lord?' Even though we could not begin to see how God could use our loss, we began to believe that somehow he would." Years later, at another church, Jerry and his wife started another support group to help people in similar situations of loss, and it ministered to people for years. Jerry is also writing his own book about his circumstances as a way of reaching out to others who can relate.

The suffering Jerry and his family endured was intense, but he believes it was not wasted. He does not pretend to know the reasons why all of it happened, but far from embittering him toward God, these dire circumstances have pushed him closer to the Lord. Jerry also believes God is now using him in ways that otherwise would not have been possible. He explains, "What I know is that God has worked in all those situations to protect us from evil, help us survive, and hold onto hope. He has also helped us use these experiences to assist and encourage others. We have somehow become part of his plan to bring healing out of heartache."

Redemption cannot be rushed; people need time to face their pain and mourn their losses.

Jerry Deans now speaks eloquently about the ways God has used the pain in his life, but it took him a long time to reach this place of understanding. "In the beginning," he said, "we were hurting so badly that we could not see God working in our situation to redeem it. Faced with the loss of a child, the permanent disability of our son, and a diagnosis of cancer, we were disturbed in every way you can be disturbed." As someone who has counseled many people going through grief, he says some mistakenly try to rush to find ways to redeem the loss. Any effort to avoid the necessary work of grief almost always backfires and leaves people frustrated. It is just as big a mistake to try to rush God's work of redemption in the aftermath of a tragedy as it is to deny it when it comes. There is no timetable.

Perhaps worse than rushing oneself, it is also a mistake to try to rush others through their grief in order to try to get them to see the redemptive aspects of their stories. Jerry said, "If there is anything we have found to be universal from those who come to our grief support groups and retreats, it is the experience of anger and exasperation in response to the 'easy answers' that are offered by well-meaning people who don't think through the impact of what they are saying."

God must have needed her in heaven more than you needed her here.

I understand what you are going through.

This must be a part of God's plan.

Everything happens for a reason.

Jerry says that, in coming up with easy answers at the point of people's most incomprehensible grief, people "misrepresent the loving God who suffers with us and longs to draw close to us when we are hurting this way." In his support groups, Jerry allows people to vent their anger at these kinds of statements, but he also urges them to see that, while the people's words may be insensitive, their intentions are usually loving. He urges those who hear such comments to look beyond the *content* of the words and think about the *intent*. People should be appreciated for reaching out in concern, even if they do so clumsily.

How can we learn to help those who are in this early stage of loss? Jerry says when he and his wife were mourning the loss of their daughter, those who helped them the most were the friends who were willing to cry with them or who shared their memories of Shantel. A friend's presence in a time of grief may mean more than any words, but if words are spoken, the most helpful kinds of comments might be ones such as, "I can't possibly fathom or begin to understand the pain you are going through right now," or, "I want to do something to help you out in some small way. If you want to talk, I'd like to listen."

In the immediate aftermath of a tragedy, the possibility of any redemptive good that might emerge from that tragedy may be beyond our imagination.

One man who has written eloquently of redemption that springs from catastrophe is Jerry Sittser, author of *A Grace Disguised* (1996) and *A Grace Revealed* (2012). In 1991 Sittser's wife, mother, and youngest daughter were all killed in a drunk-driving accident. His first book about the redemptive aftermath of this tragedy came out a few years after the accident, but he wrote his most recent book twenty years after, having had more time to reflect. It has taken him that long to see the full ramifications of God's redemptive work, and his story is still unfolding.

The idea that adversity produces character may sound fine in abstract terms, but Sittser never wanted to test that idea in reality. He says, "In truth, I would have liked to remain a spoiled child."[4] The deaths of his family members removed that option. He was forced to face stark reality. But he says it took many years before he could see any good emerge from the accident, in terms of its producing any character or other good in himself or his children. Nor was he really even looking for such a redemptive outcome. He preferred the life he had lost and wanted only to return to those relationships and the world of the past.

Although God's redemptive work was not immediately apparent to Sittser, he began over time to see more and more clearly the evidence of God's work in his family's life. He says they simply had to give God "the room to work and try our best to maintain faith when there didn't appear to be much reason to. Looking back some twenty years later, I can only express utter astonishment at what God has done. It makes me almost grateful for the loss itself, which I find incomprehensible."[5]

The passage of time was a key aspect of Sittser's remarkable change of perspective, but what he did during those twenty years also made a big difference. Instead of allowing his pain to turn to bitterness or hopelessness, he hung on to his faith and gave God time to work, even when his own imagination could see no way out of the pain. At our lowest moments, simply clinging to God— even as we cry out to him and blame him and scream in agony in his presence—may be our most courageous act of faith.

As the psalmists knew, God is not offended or threatened by our cries of anguish, even when those cries include our complaints against God. There is not much restraint in the psalms of lament, in which the speaker cries out things like:

"My soul is in deep anguish. How long, LORD, how long?" (Psalm 6:3)

"Will you forget me forever? How long will you hide your face from me? How long must I wrestle with my thoughts and every day have sorrow in my heart?" (Psalm 13:1b-2a)

"I cry aloud to the LORD; I lift up my voice to the LORD for mercy. I pour out before him my complaint; before him I tell my trouble" (Psalm 142:1-2).

In the midst of these desperate pleas, the psalmist stays *connected* to God. The Lord may take a long time to accomplish his rescue, but the psalmist gives no thought to cutting himself off from his relationship or trust in God, even when he can't understand why God won't end the suffering.

Even if a full understanding of God's redemptive purposes in tragedy never comes in this life, hints of redemption often appear even in the worst moments.

As Jerry Sittser's books show, the redemptive aspects of his tragic story have taken many years to become evident. However, he also describes hints of the coming redemption that emerged even during the agonizing ride in the ambulance right after he had witnessed the deaths of his family members. As he sat there, a chorus of Scripture floated through his mind:

Echo after echo, like a chorus of biblical voices. Sitting in the ambulance, I discover that the tragic story into which we have been thrust is enveloped by another story. The accident, however random, does not stand on its own or exist unto itself. It is part of a larger story. In that moment, I have no idea how; that is for me to discover in the future. For now, in the painful silence, it is enough to know there is a story out there that can make sense of my own. But it is not merely *a* story; it is *the* story.[6]

The story he is referring to is God's ultimate story of redemption through Jesus Christ. It would be years before Sittser understood the full implications of how his own story fit that larger story, but in the meantime, hints like the "chorus of biblical voices" kept him leaning in the Lord's direction.

Smaller crises may also challenge and change us in significant ways.

Many people never face the extreme disasters like those that Jerry Deans or Jerry Sittser endured, in which family members are suddenly killed or severely harmed in an accident, changing the family's life forever. Instead, many people sense that their lives have been hobbled by problems that are less dramatic but that, nonetheless, make their days difficult to endure. These problems may be illnesses or disabilities or unfortunate circumstances that may look minor to others. People may feel reluctant even to complain aloud about these problems since, compared to the major ordeals that others suffer, their own problems look insignificant.

When I read Sittser's book *A Grace Revealed*, written twenty years after the accident that killed his mother, wife, and daughter, I was surprised when I came across a passage in which he says, "Adversity does not have to be dramatic to have an effect. Strangely, I realize now that it has not been the grandiose events of suffering that have proven to be so difficult for me but the lesser disappointments along the way that have eroded my spirit, sapped my energy, and put me to the test."[7] As examples, he mentions times when his computer froze and he lost something important that he hadn't saved, or when he faced the stress of taking care of his kids when they got sick all at the same time. Sometimes he found seemingly small things pushing him over the edge.

Why would a man who had suffered some of the worst blows life could throw at a person be so bothered by these comparatively insignificant problems? He says, "The insignificance of it was in fact the problem. All of us face dozens of moments just like it every day; the impact is always cumulative, eventually wearing us down like dripping water erodes solid rock. Mundane adversity, like any other kind, reminds us that we are not in control."[8]

Even though many of us would look at Sittser's story and consider his tragedy extreme, he does not put his own suffering in a different category than what everybody else faces. "Mine was no more severe than others," he writes. "For example, I never had to face rejection; I never had to care for a loved one with permanent disabilities; I never had to absorb one loss after another, the first setting off a chain reaction, with many more to follow."[9]

I can relate to Sittser's idea that the seemingly small adversities can be more disruptive at times than the big ones. When I am faced with the big disasters, I often *realize* it is a moment of challenge, and I can steel myself with the strength, prayer, and help from others that I will need to get through it. With the smaller challenges, I may feel alone, misunderstood, and unsupported.

I may not even acknowledge that I'm in a situation in which I am being tested until I have already lost my temper or given in to dejection. Those around me also may not see what I'm going through as anything to be worried about, so they don't bother to reach out to help.

For many of us, what is most frustrating about the smaller ordeals is their seeming pointlessness. We would be willing to suffer for our faith and sacrifice for God if only we could see that it served some big purpose. We have the capacity for large acts of heroism, but to be nitpicked to death by the annoying drip-drip-drip of everyday suffering merely leaves us feeling humiliated and alone. Kathleen Anderson, the former powerlifter and runner, commented on that difficulty of suffering in ways that sap our endurance but don't seem to advance the kingdom of God: "As Christians, we know that we must take up our crosses and follow him daily. But what happens when that cross is gallbladder failure or an allergy to tomatoes? Saints in ages past were boiled in oil or crucified upside down for their faith. What good is it to suffer as an unwilling martyr merely to one's own brittle body?"[10]

Anderson and Sittser both ultimately conclude that these difficult but unspectacular, or un-heroic, struggles *do* serve a redemptive purpose. Anderson believes her physical struggles have made her more empathetic to others in pain, more aware of God's presence in the midst of her suffering, and more aware of the illusion of self-reliance and the reality of her dependence on God. Sittser focuses on the choices these everyday adversities force us to make: "Will we stay on our own course and continue to be our old self, which adversity exposes as small and petty, impatient and angry, irritable and ungrateful? Or will we choose the course God sets and become a different kind of person, one characterized by love for God and neighbor, goodness of heart, and godliness of character?"[11]

No adversity, no matter how small, or how annoying, or how humiliating, needs to be wasted. God can use any of it to push us closer toward the kind of people he wants us to be. In an article in *Today's Christian Woman,* my friend Karen O'Connor showed how even a woman's severe case of shingles was redeemed in ways beyond what she and her family could have imagined. The woman afflicted with shingles could not tolerate pain medication, and her condition was so bad that she was bedridden for a year, suffering terrible pain the whole time. She lost twenty pounds, and she also lost her independence, which had always meant so much to her.

Her illness was a torment for her in every way, but the pain was not wasted. In her seventies, she had been estranged from her daughter for years. In desperation, she began to call her daughter several times a day, asking for prayer. Gradually, their relationship was restored. The illness also brought the woman closer to her husband of sixty-two years. He closed his office when she got sick and devoted himself to taking care of her. The daughter watched as her parents' marriage grew in love and respect. The husband said, "The love your mother and I have for each other has reached greater heights than anything I could have imagined during previous years."[12]

God can redeem tragic circumstances in an endless number of ways. God can use disaster to change people's perspectives, their priorities, their relationships, and their very place and purpose in the universe. Although each person's situation is unique in certain ways, I have noticed one element that almost everyone has in common when they allow redemption to spring from their pain: Redemption is almost never about one person alone. Others are also touched in significant ways by what happens to the person who has suffered.

Go to beaconhillbooks.com/go/nothingiswasted for a free downloadable study guide that includes questions for deeper personal reflection as well as activities for use in a small group setting.

3 ❦ YOUR SUFFERING IS NOT ONLY ABOUT YOU

In almost every case I have seen in which people reported that their pain ultimately was not wasted, part of that redemption was that other people were brought into their stories and were somehow helped in ways that would not have been possible if the disaster had not occurred. Often the people who are helped the most are those who show up to help the person through the tragedy.

Eleven years, almost to the day, after the death of Jerry Deans's daughter Shantel, his sixteen-year-old twin sons, Matthew and Mark, suffered a terrible car accident. Matthew sustained an injury to his spine. Although surgeons did what they could to help the athletic young runner, on the day after the surgery, the doctors delivered the terrible news that Matthew was unlikely ever to walk unassisted again. The best he could hope for was to be able to walk with crutches or a walker someday, but he would most likely spend the rest of his life in a wheelchair.

The news hit Jerry and his family hard. Beyond their sorrow over their son's condition and the lifelong challenges he would face, this latest blow simply seemed like more than the family should have to bear. Jerry said, "I'd like to be able to say that I never once throughout this experience doubted God or wondered, *Why us, Lord? Haven't we already had our share of heartache and tragedy?* This seemed so cruel."

The family had been on a long road toward healing after Shantel's death and the subsequent tragedies of eleven years earlier. Now this? Jerry had not expected to have to deal with something of this magnitude again. As he put it, "We had convinced ourselves that our bad luck was behind us. After all, the number and succession of losses we had experienced were rare. The odds were now in our favor, right?"

Like the string of misfortunes that accompanied Shantel's death, Matthew's tragedy ushered in another year of painful events. The month after Matthew's accident, Jerry's mother died. In December of that year, his son Jamie underwent an emergency appendectomy. In February of the next year, the family learned that Matthew's twin brother, Mark, had a serious but previously undetected injury from the July car accident. On the same day Jerry found out the news about Mark, he also learned some scary news about himself: He had been diagnosed with prostate cancer.

As the suffering increased, however, so did the opportunities for people's lives to be changed in positive ways. Without any orchestration from Jerry or his family, word of Matthew's accident spread, and before long, churches across Virginia, Alabama, Tennessee, Indiana, and elsewhere throughout the country began praying. Matthew received so many cards and letters at the hospital that one day one of the mail room employees stopped by his room simply so he could see the "celebrity" who was receiving so much mail.

Jerry says of this season that "God's presence was conspicuous. He was in this with us, and not just holding our hands saying, *There, there; everything will be okay.* He was moving, touching, inspiring, activating, transforming, and dragging us along, completely caught up in the mystery and wonder of it all."

One practical problem the family faced in caring for Matthew was that all three bedrooms and both bathrooms of their home were on the second floor, which would not work well for Matthew's wheelchair. Jerry and Patsi decided they would have to sell their home and move somewhere else. When Jerry called his real estate agent, Helen, who was a friend and a member of his church, and explained the situation, she said she would look into what other houses might be available.

The next weekend, however, when Jerry called to see what progress she had made, she stunned him by declaring, "Jerry, you don't have to sell your house. The church is going to help." A fund had been set up to pay for an addition to Jerry's house that would accommodate Matthew's needs, and church members had committed to donate time, labor, skills, and money in order to make it happen.

When Jerry protested that he couldn't ask the church to take on something that big, Helen responded, "Jerry, the church needs to do this as much as you need it to be done."

Jerry was skeptical. Their church had been experiencing some internal conflict, so he wondered whether this would really be the right time for them to take on such a big project. "But," he says, "God saw it differently. For him, it was perfect timing, and confirmation began flooding in."

People volunteered their services in every area of the project—architecture and design, construction, electrical work, plumbing, tree removal, meals for the workers, and the list went on. "Whenever there was a day when we needed help," said Jerry, "that help would show up in just the right numbers, with just the right skills. On one Monday evening when we were framing and needed a lot of assistance, fifteen people just dropped by. I remember coming home some evenings after working late, and I couldn't even find a place to park my car."

When the work was finished, Jerry's house had a new, 900-square-foot wing designed to match the rest of the house. It contained a wheelchair-accessible bedroom, living area, closet, and bathroom for Matthew. A ramp connected the new wing to the driveway.

"Matthew returned to a hero's welcome," said Jerry.

Matthew's pain, and that of his family, was deep and regrettable, but it was not wasted. What happened in the aftermath of the accident was transformative not only for Matthew but also for Jerry, for his family, for the church members who joined together to help someone in need, and for dozens of people across several states who united in prayer and wrote cards and letters. Jerry and his family had to allow others into their suffering, and once they did, love flowed in.

One Woman Suffers, but Thousands Are Touched

When I first met Amy Hauser, three years after her original diagnosis of breast cancer, some of the things she had endured include: a bilateral mastectomy and reconstructive surgeries, chemotherapy, periods of "chemo brain" fuzziness and confusion, loss of all her hair (and the stares from others that her hair loss triggered), sleeplessness, endless doctor's appointments, fear of what might happen next, weakness, weariness, temporarily worsened eyesight, terrible back pain, and other problems.

Although Amy's breast cancer brought suffering into her life that was beyond anything she had experienced before, it also changed her and hundreds of others in ways she never could have anticipated.

Early on in their ordeal, Amy and her husband, Tom, realized that their pain and the unexpected blessings that flowed from it were not theirs alone. Their children, their church, and many people they would never know were drawn into their story and were helped and inspired. Before Amy first discovered the lump that would lead to her life-threatening and ultimately life-changing journey, the main problem on her mind was her fraying marriage. After twenty years, she and Tom felt frustrated and dissatisfied with each other, and they were both ready to give up.

One day, months before her discovery of cancer, Amy plopped down on a park bench and prayed about what to do in her marriage. The message that came clearly to her mind was, *Wait one year.* That was not what she wanted or expected to hear, but she felt certain that's what the Lord was telling her. That prayer took place in September. The following May, Amy discovered she had breast cancer. Following that diagnosis, her life was completely disrupted, in both good ways and bad.

First, of course, came the bad. Amy was afraid. She had two children, in eighth grade and fourth grade. How could she tell them she had cancer? What might this mean for them? Would she live? Even if she did, how much would this battle take her away from her family, how much would it sap her strength, and what new burdens and worries would it place on her husband and kids? Would Tom be up to the challenge? Would their troubled marriage crumble under the weight of this new crisis? The family had only recently moved from Iowa to Texas, and were still adjusting to their new home and new church. Would Amy find the friendship and support she needed?

Even though she had more questions than answers, and even though she faced lots of pain and endless hassles and disruptions, Amy sensed God's presence very close to her from the start. She wrote, "It was a dark unknown place, yet not as terrifying as I might have thought. I didn't know then, and am just starting to realize now, that my Shepherd was...taking me by the hand and clearly leading me into a different battleground, yet letting me know he was going to see me through and guide me to the other side."[1]

Amy and Tom kept an online journal of their experience, which they later turned into the book *In His Grip: A Walk through Breast Cancer.* Their site received more than eighteen thousand visits over the course of Amy's treatment, with more than eight hundred guestbook entries from people offering prayers and encouragement. Made for More Ministries (*made4moreministries.com*), which began during this time, continues today.

One of the first positive transformations that sprang from Amy's diagnosis was the revival of her marriage. Amy's crisis united the couple more strongly than ever before. As Amy put it,

It didn't take long to see that Tom was being carried and equipped to handle the huge task at hand as husband and father, to name just a few of the many roles that a caretaker must shoulder. God was the equipper, no doubt... When faced with cancer, the acceptance that we were not perfect, but that we were a family and it was time to pull together, really came to the surface... Trusting the Father and accepting that he would work both on us and in us to stick together as a family, through thick and thin, was not easy. It has worked better than any therapy ever could have, though.[2]

Many details of Tom and Amy's renewed love for each other could be drawn from their story, but one incident that illustrates it vividly happened on a day when Amy was at her lowest, so weak that she was in bed 85 percent of the time, her whole body aching. By this time she had lost her hair and had to shave her head occasionally. In a journal entry she wrote, "Tom gave me another shave today. He is so gentle. He has gotten really fast and good with the old razor. It is very cool to have your husband love you enough to shave your head. I love him so much. He is such a compassionate provider for all of us. I am blessed."[3]

Amy's ordeal also brought growth and change in her children. With Amy unable to function in many of the ways she was used to, her children had to learn more independence. They also learned the ability to see beyond their own needs and put the needs of a hurting person before themselves. Before this crisis, Amy had tried to shield the children from difficulty, but she later realized that her kids grew through this trial in ways they would not have grown without it.

Hundreds of other people have been touched in a positive way because of Amy's struggle with cancer. Beyond those who followed her story and interacted with her online, many others helped her in practical ways. In one journal entry she thanked friends for the outpouring of cards, prayers, notes, and food. At that moment her freezer contained "about a dozen serving size soups ready to go, a pot of chicken enchilada soup, dessert, barbecue, salad and other food I can't remember, all having been delivered to our door."[4]

Creating Beauty Out of Brokenness: Mosaics

Even in the midst of her illness, as Amy suffered from general weakness and the "chemo brain" mental fuzziness that was a side effect of her treatment, she found ways to minister to others. One aspect of her ministry was teaching kids to make tile mosaics at a Cowkids day camp. The children at her retreats, many of them from troubled backgrounds, broke up tiles and pots as Amy taught them that the pieces represented the broken aspects of life, bad things that happen such as divorce, death, or other losses. Faced with those difficulties, everyone has choices about what to do with the broken pieces.

The canvas on which the tiles were glued represented the young artists' lives. They could choose what they wanted to do with their canvases and their broken pieces. They could see the shards as trash and throw them away, or they could use them to make something beautiful. The process, in life and in art, is messy. It takes time. When the mortar is dumped on the broken pieces, the whole thing may look like nothing but a disaster, but careful hands can smooth it and shape it into something pleasing that never could have existed if the pieces had remained whole.

By the time I met Amy Hauser at a writers conference, her cancer treatments were complete, and she had regained her hair and her energy. But the redemptive elements of her story continued. She was working on her book, speaking in many venues, and conducting operations for Made for More Ministries with Tom.

Good May Spring from Disaster, but the Pain Never Leaves

For Amy Hauser, Jerry Deans, and many others whose stories I have encountered, it occurs to me how easy it would have been for them to have *blocked* the redemption that sprang from their ordeals. If they had decided to suffer alone, to collapse inward in despair, or to harden themselves against God's presence, they might have experienced only heartache that would have led to nothing good for themselves or for anyone else.

Their openness to God and others rescued not only them but also those who helped them. They developed new relationships that enriched their lives. They used their suffering as a springboard to love others. Thousands of people have benefited from that vulnerability. Like the mosaics that Amy's students created, beauty sprang from broken and ugly circumstances—but only because they allowed it to.

Even with the most miraculous redeeming circumstances, people never get over blows like the loss of a child or the memory of the physical pain of a near-death illness or the humiliation of financial disaster or the sting of other great losses. Tragedy and redemption do not exist as an equation in which one side equals or cancels out the other. In some cases, the tragedy may appear to far outweigh any redeeming counterforces that spring from it, while in other cases the redemption may seem to more than make up for the suffering endured.

About a year after Amy Hauser's final chemotherapy session, bilateral mastectomy, and reconstructive surgeries in her fight against life-threatening, strength-sapping breast cancer, she made a statement that many would find astonishing. She wrote, "From where I stand, I wouldn't trade my experience, starting with that phone call...revealing that I had breast cancer, for whatever would have happened if the news had been that my cancer screenings had come back clear."[5]

Think of that. She would not trade that horrible experience for a much easier life that might have been given to her instead. "Without that call," she said, "I know I would not have had the drive to live life from a new perspective—seeing each day as an opportunity rather than a hassle or a burden, and focusing on the blessings rather than on what is lacking."[6] Amy prays she never has to experience any of this again, but she sees that it served a purpose. Her marriage, which was on the brink of disaster, is now strong because of the way the crisis brought her and Tom back together. It also awakened her to a new outlook on life and spurred her desire to minister to others who are in pain.

Not everyone who suffers would go as far as Amy does in saying that they would not trade their catastrophes for easier lives. Even many of those who clearly see the ways God has used the suffering in their lives to change them for the better and to minister to others still see the cost of their own suffering as so high that they would have done anything to avoid it. When I asked Jerry Deans about this, he said that he and his wife have never come to terms enough with their losses to contemplate the idea of gratitude that they happened. "Even though it is clear that God has redeemed our losses," he said, "we would still gladly give up the positive impact it has had on us and others in trade for the life of our daughter, who had wonderful potential for raising and teaching children. Or the able body of our son, who suffers each day with pain, sleeplessness, and countless symptoms stemming from spinal cord injury. Or, in my case, freedom from the threat of cancer as well as the numerous side effects of treatment that are now a part of my life."

Of course, these responses are all hypothetical, since no one *does* get a choice in these adversities that strike. They hit when people least expect them, and the sufferer's only choice is how to respond. Even the choice of how to respond is not unlimited. In the short run, grief, confusion, and anger may be the only realistic responses for people in some dire situations. It is only over time, as people begin to work through the raw emotions and see hints of God's redemptive purposes, that they may have an increasing amount of choice about how much they will allow God's transforming power into their circumstances.

Jerry Deans has had many years to work through his continued relationship with God in the midst of an unusual degree of suffering. He does not believe God caused his tragedies in order to achieve some plan. God has allowed these things to happen, and Jerry has trusted God enough to work creatively with him to bring redemption out of them. Jerry has *chosen* persistence in faith and has chosen not to blame God for the bad things that happened. He believes ultimately that God will not fail him, even if that means pain sometimes prevails in the short term.

Go to beaconhillbooks.com/go/nothingiswasted for a free downloadable study guide that includes questions for deeper personal reflection as well as activities for use in a small group setting.

4 ✒ THE GOD OF
THE IMPOSSIBLE

God is creative. God is bizarre. As I have studied the ways he pulls good things from dire circumstances, I have noticed he often does it in ways that are so roundabout and unexpected that the people could never have known to ask for them. These ways seem to have God's fingerprints on them because they are too unusual to have come about in any other way. It is often as if God wants to rescue a situation but only when it has reached the point where a favorable outcome looks impossible. He is the God of the impossible.

When a Young Mother's Death Is Not the End of the Story

One example of God's eccentric way of redeeming a situation began with what looked like a denied prayer. Its result was the death of a young mother of four children. The woman's husband was devastated, her children were left without a mother, and a church who had poured itself into prayer for her was left disappointed in God's lack of response.

That death was not the end of the story. God had other plans.

When I first met Sandi Welborn at a writers conference in North Carolina, she was the picture of contentment—a friendly, soft-spoken Southern woman whose life was filled with lots of time with her children and grandchildren and travels with her husband. The story she had brought to the conference to get into shape revealed a background with more complications and adversity than anyone might have guessed by looking at Sandi's life now. In fact, her struggle started even before she was born. When Sandi's mother found out at the age of fifteen that she was pregnant with Sandi, her parents (Sandi's grandparents) urged her to have an abortion. The only way she avoided it was to run off and marry the father of the baby.

They raised Sandi in southern California, where her father worked at Lockheed in Long Beach. On the outside they might have looked like any typical, middle-class American family, but that façade covered a harsher reality. Her father often gambled away his paycheck, and her mother often felt frustrated, trapped, too young to be raising a family.

Eventually the family split; Sandi's brother went with their father, and Sandi stayed with her mother. Divorce and an angry custody battle soon followed. Then, when Sandi was eight years old, her life took an even more tragic turn. One day, in the midst of the custody battle, her father showed up at the house and asked to see Sandi's mother. Sandi told him her mother was at the store but would be back soon. Her father did not stay but told Sandi to tell his ex-wife she had won, and she now had the kids. He said goodbye and drove away.

The next morning, a policeman came to the door to say that Sandi's father had committed suicide, in a park nearby, not long after his final conversation with his daughter.

Sandi's mother remarried, and the family moved to San Diego. Sandi became a Christian there, and by the time she was in her early twenties, she was a passionate believer who went to church at every opportunity, and she became deeply involved in the church's singles group. She also became good friends with the pastor's daughter and was often invited to her home. There she grew close to the pastor's wife, Peggy, who mentored Sandi spiritually and also talked to her about her dating life. Peggy encouraged Sandi to believe that God had a plan for her life. She even thought Sandi herself might make a good pastor's wife. Sandi didn't see herself that way but was happy that Peggy thought highly enough of her to say so.

Sandi learned about intercessory prayer one evening when she was at Peggy's home and the phone rang. Sandi listened as Peggy took the phone call, which was obviously some kind of bad news. After Peggy listened to the story and asked some questions, she began to pray through her tears for a young woman who had been reported to be gravely ill with cancer. After the call, Peggy told Sandi that the woman, Becky, and her husband, Allen, had been stationed at the nearby airbase and had gone to their church but had moved to North Carolina, where Allen had become a minister. Now Becky had a tumor in her stomach that was inoperable. The couple had four children. The situation was desperate, and only prayer and God's intervention could save her.

The whole church began to pray for this young woman and her family. Sandi got so involved in praying for her that she felt she almost knew Becky. As the weeks went by and the prayer continued, Sandi felt sure that God would answer these prayers and spare the life of this woman whose husband and children so relied on her.

Instead, the woman died. When Sandi heard the announcement of Becky's death, she says, "A shadow of sadness went deeper into my heart than I had ever felt before. It was not just the passing of this young mother that caused me to grieve. It was also the first time I had felt as though God had let me down. I had truly believed God was going to heal her. What happened?"

One thing Sandi did not know is that Becky, a few thousand miles away, had prayed a much different kind of prayer not long before she died. Lying in her hospital room and sensing that the hundreds of prayers for her healing would not be answered, Becky prayed, "Lord, my heart is so heavy, my time is short; please hear my prayer. I need the assurance that you will send a mother for my children and a loving wife for my husband."

Sandi felt a nagging disappointment and sadness for weeks after Becky's death. Even though she had never even met her, the intense intercessory prayer in which Sandi had participated had made her feel close to Becky. Sandi didn't want to question God's wisdom, but she couldn't understand why he hadn't healed Becky.

A few weeks later, on a Sunday morning, Sandi entered the choir room for practice and learned that the church had a special guest that morning. Becky's husband, Allen, was visiting. The church had taken up an offering to pay for the grieving minister to travel from North Carolina to California to have a few days of rest.

This visiting minister looked much different from what Sandi had pictured as she prayed for him and Becky. She had never seen a picture of him, but she knew he was thirty-two, which to her, at age twenty-three, had sounded pretty old. Her experience with what ministers looked like was also pretty limited, but most of the ones she had seen tended toward the solemn, scholarly, black-suit-and-tie look. After all he had been through, she expected him to look haggard, and for reasons she couldn't even explain, she had pictured him short and pudgy.

Allen was none of those things. Sandi said she will never forget her first encounter with him on that day in 1982. As she sat in the choir loft while the service began, she saw Allen on the platform standing next to her pastor. Rather than the dour, frazzled figure she had pictured, Allen was tall, youthful, handsome, and well-dressed in a sport coat and tie. "Yes, it's true my heart did flutter," says Sandi. "He was very handsome. For a brief moment, I forgot the tragedy that had brought this man to our church."

She was further impressed when Allen spoke to the congregation, thanking them for their support of his family during their difficult days. He reaffirmed his trust in God, saying, "The past several months have been very hard for us. Becky's passing was a great loss. God has been so good to my children and me through it all. I have no doubt that God has a plan for my family. Becky's passing did not come as a surprise to God. I am determined that my family and I are going to trust him for the future."

Although Sandi did not yet know it, she was to be part of that future.

Happily Ever After, Or...?

You see where this is headed, don't you? Sandi ended up marrying Allen, but that first morning when they met was all about awkwardness rather than romance. As Sandi made her way down from the choir loft at the end of the service, Peggy stopped her—as a group of friends stood by listening—and said she wanted to make sure Sandi met Allen because she had told him all about her. Sandi realized Peggy was trying to fix them up, and all the listening friends, to Sandi's embarrassment, started offering their own encouragement for this idea.

Sandi wanted to run away. It was one thing to secretly admire Allen from the anonymity of the choir loft, but now she felt as if the whole church were conspiring behind her back. She says, "I just stood there with a half smile on my face, trying to be polite, while inside feeling horrified by the fact that they had already begun trying to fix this poor man up." She slipped out of the church as quickly as she could before anyone could introduce her to Allen, who was still greeting people at the front of the church.

Then came the evening service, where Sandi once again had to make a quick exit to avoid being shoved in front of Allen. She was determined to keep a low profile later that evening at the restaurant where many of the church people gathered after the service. However, before she could find an inconspicuous place in the back of the restaurant, she suddenly found herself face to face with the young pastor, who introduced himself and invited her to sit at his table.

The two felt an instant connection, but Sandi wished their meeting wasn't happening under the gaze of the entire congregation. What did everyone expect? It was Sunday night, and by Thursday Allen would be gone, traveling the couple thousand miles back to his four children in North Carolina.

Still, the next several days offered several opportunities for Sandi and Allen to be together, in groups of people and, finally, alone. He invited her to lunch on the day before he was to leave. When the conversation turned serious, Allen surprised her with the question, "What would you think of being the mother of four children and moving to another state?"

Describing her reaction to that blunt question, Sandi now says, "Surprisingly, I didn't faint or allow my mouth to drop wide open; I didn't even sprint for the exit. As strange as it may sound, I knew he wasn't asking me to marry him, but rather I had a sense he was wanting to know if there was an open door to explore the future."

He was leaving the next day. There was no time for game-playing.

Sandi's answer to him was, "Well, I guess if that's what the Lord has in store for me, I'd be fine with it."

She says now, "The smile that spread across his face was one I'll never forget. We sat in silence, our eyes locked on each other, just smiling. The silence this time was anything but awkward."

Allen went back to North Carolina, and Sandi was left to contemplate the head-spinning circumstances that had led her to this point.

Imagine yourself in Sandi's situation. When she prayed for Allen and his wife, Becky, having never met them, she truly believed God would heal Becky and allow her to get back to raising her four children. After all, that seemed like the most sensible and compassionate solution. Why had God not done it?

It was impossible to answer that, and now Sandi faced the possibility that her entire future was tied to God's refusal to grant the request to save the life of this young mother. The situation was filled with an undeniable strangeness, but how should Sandi respond? Was it simply too bizarre to believe that God was somehow involved in using her to bring something good out of this tragic event? Did she even want such disruption? If things worked out with Allen, she would go from being a single woman in California to a wife and mother of four children in North Carolina overnight.

How Often Does God Do the Impossible?

Does God really work in such roundabout ways to pull redemption from tragedy? If the Bible is any indication, then the answer is undoubtedly yes. Start from the end of almost any Bible story and ask yourself whether the outcome emerges in the most straightforward way. Take Jacob, the great Old Testament patriarch whose sons become the heads of the twelve tribes of Israel. Does he achieve his status in the most straightforward way? Ask Esau, his brother, who is tricked out of his birthright by Jacob. Or ask Jacob's father, Isaac, whom Jacob also fools. A terrible situation of deceit and injustice, yet redemption somehow manages to wind its way through this story, with Jacob ending up in a place to play a key role in the formation of the Israelites.

What about those twelve sons who are to lead the twelve tribes of Israel? Is that simply a clear-cut matter of Jacob getting married and having one son after another until all twelve are in place? Not even close. Jacob the trickster falls in love with Rachel, but her father makes Jacob work for him for seven years before he can marry her. That sounds harsh enough, but when the seven years are up and the wedding day finally arrives, Jacob marries the love of his life, only to lift up her veil and find out he has actually married Rachel's sister, Leah! Then he has to work another seven years to finally marry Rachel.

Now Jacob has two wives, and this whole dysfunctional background does not create a harmonious household in which to raise the future leaders of the twelve tribes of Israel. Leah gives birth to the first four children, much to Rachel's disappointment. Rachel, unable to conceive but not wanting to be left childless while her sister continues to produce children, persuades Jacob to have children through her maid, Bilhah, which seems weird to us but is somewhat normal in their culture. Bilhah gives birth to two children, but then Leah responds by talking Jacob into having two children with *her* maid, Zilpah. Are you following this? That makes a total of eight children so far. Leah follows this by giving birth to three more children—two boys and a girl. Rachel, way behind in this unhappy competition, finally conceives and gives birth to Joseph. Rachel later becomes pregnant again—are her prospects for happiness finally improving? She gives birth to Benjamin, but then she dies in childbirth.

Thus is the foundation laid for Israel's great tribal leaders. And that only accounts for how they are born, leaving out the tremendous amount of drama and conflict that still lie ahead. Looking at these details, one might be tempted to predict that God's whole plan will fall apart, but it doesn't. In spite of trickery, disobedience, revenge, and many other barriers, God runs a thread of redemption throughout this story and many others. He fulfills his intentions in the midst of the messes people create.

And that is only one of dozens of examples the Bible offers of God working out his purposes in ways that at first look as if they could never turn out well. I could talk about Joseph in a pit, or Jeremiah in a pit, or Jonah in the belly of a fish, or Paul in multiple prisons, or Moses in a desert, or many other weird circumstances. Judging by Scripture, the bizarre becomes the norm when it comes to ways in which God's designs are fulfilled.

So when Sandi considered whether she might become a redemptive answer to the plight of the young pastor and his four children who had lost their wife and mother, whose own dying prayer had been that God would provide a loving wife for her husband and a loving mother for her children, did it really seem so unusual?

With Allen back in North Carolina with his four children and Sandi a couple thousand miles away in California, there was every possibility that their short acquaintance would simply fade away and be forgotten. This was the early 1980s, well before the advent of social media, instant messaging, or texting. Allen and Sandi had two ways to communicate—the telephone (with long-distance charges) and the postal service—and they spent lots of time and money on both over the following weeks. They spent hours on the phone getting to know each other and regularly wrote letters that deepened their relationship. Two months after his first visit, Allen surprised Sandi by announcing that he was flying back to California to see her.

By the end of Allen's five-day trip, the couple knew they were in love. Sandi says, "I felt sure the Lord was at work in our relationship. I just knew together we could have a wonderful life. I also felt like there was nothing in life that we could face that would stop us from loving each other. I had fallen hard."

Not everyone, however, was happy about this budding relationship. Some friends and family of both worried that things were moving too quickly. Sandi was too much in love to pay much attention, and Allen was moving forward in spite of what anyone said. He invited Sandi to come to North Carolina the next month.

Sandi was nervous about meeting Allen's children, his congregation, and his other friends and family. He had prepared his children for this visitor, and from the beginning, they were open and friendly to her. The visit went well. People were welcoming, and as the days passed, Sandi became increasingly convinced that marrying Allen was the right thing to do. She loved him, and she also quickly felt close to the children. "From the moment I walked into Allen's home," Sandi says, "God began to give me a desire to fill the void that had been left behind by Becky's passing. As I got to know each one of the children, they became precious in their own way. The thought of being their mom didn't seem like just a good idea; it felt almost natural."

Before her trip was over, Allen gave Sandi an engagement ring, and the couple set a wedding date.

New Love Springs from Tragedy—But It's Complicated

Allen and Sandi saw their marriage as a redemptive gift that sprang from the tragedy of Becky's death. They saw it as an answer to Becky's final prayer. But during the first months of their marriage, Sandi sometimes had to endure unkind comments from people who thought Allen had remarried too quickly, or whose grief over Becky's loss made it difficult for them to accept Sandi as Allen's wife.

In particular, Becky's mother, Nadine, was devastated over the loss of her daughter, and she was devoted to her four grandchildren. Her relationship with Sandi did not begin well. The main way Sandi felt Nadine's displeasure was through criticism of San-di's parenting skills. Sandi was young and inexperienced at raising children, and now she was suddenly raising four of them. Nadine's list of complaints, often mentioned through seemingly casual comments to Allen, was long. Sandi didn't know how to cook the Southern foods the kids liked, she packed the wrong clothes for their trips to their grandmother's house, she forgot to make them brush their teeth after meals, and many other things. Sandi was already insecure about her lack of experience as a mother, so even when the criticisms were accurate, they weren't helpful.

At Allen's urging, Sandi decided it was up to her to reach out to Nadine to try to break through the barrier that stood between them. With trepidation she made the phone call to set up a meet-ing between just the two of them. At first it went like any other meeting between them, with Nadine picking away with little re-minders of things Sandi should be doing for the children. Sandi finally shifted the conversation to directly confront the issue be-fore them. She wanted to find a way that the two of them could get along better. She knew she had a lot to learn as a mother. She knew Nadine must be hurting terribly over the loss of her daugh-ter. Now that she had gotten to know the children, Sandi could tell what a wonderful mother Becky had been.

Sandi squirmed with awkwardness as she spoke, and at first, Nadine was not receptive, but as the conversation continued, something changed. Nadine softened, and before long, she also began to talk about what a loving mother Becky had been and how much she missed her. One story led to another, and the tears flowed from both. They talked about Becky's life and also about her horrible illness and death. It was a sad conversation, but it was also one in which the two women found common ground.

As they spoke, Nadine revealed more about Becky's final prayer. It had happened two days before her death. She was very weak, but at about two in the morning she had a sudden burst of energy and was able to talk to her mother, who was in the room alone with her. They talked about each of the children, and Becky said, "Mom, I've really struggled to understand why God would take me away from my children and Allen. They need me so much." But then she added, "I want you to know God has finally given me the peace and assurance I've been asking for. God is going to send a mother for my children and a wife for Allen. When she comes, I want you to know she is here because I asked God to send her."

Though still stricken with grief, Nadine now said to Sandi, "She didn't say your name, but she was so confident that you were coming, it was as if she already knew you."

Sandi's relationship with Nadine changed after that conversation. They became closer as the years went by. At first the children were the basis of their relationship, but as time went on they also became friends.

Although four children were a handful, Sandi and Allen added a child of their own to the family. Thirty years later, their lives are rich with love from these five children and their thirteen grandchildren, each one a symbol of God's loving work in their lives. They also lead a ministry called The Right Blend that conducts marriage and family conferences at churches around the country. More about their story and their ministry can be found at *therightblend.org.*

Only God Can Save You—But Will He?

God seems to love impossible situations. The Bible goes out of its way to show people caught in situations so dire that nothing could save them, and yet *God rescues them anyway.*

If you want to find two biblical figures who face one impossibility after another, look no further than Abraham and Sarah.

They find themselves caught in such predicaments that God is their *only* hope, so they pour all their trust in him, even when circumstances make it look absurd to do so.

How is Abraham, the great hero of the faith, described in the faith chapter of Hebrews 11? He is called "as good as dead" when God finally makes a big move in his life.

Abraham is one of God's most favored people. The Lord calls him to a new land and promises to make his name great, to make him a blessing, and to bless all of the people of the earth through him and his offspring. You might think that if God were that much on his side and so eager to do big things through him, he would treat Abraham carefully and protect him from needless confusion and hassle and heartache.

Yet Abraham finds nothing but trouble.

Start with that opening promise. Abram, as he then is called, is already seventy-five years old, and his wife, Sarai, is in her sixties when that promise is made, hardly the ideal time of life to start a family. That's where the "as good as dead" phrase comes in from Hebrews. How will God pull off that part of the promise? He doesn't say (and Abram doesn't ask). God also doesn't even tell Abram where he is going. Those are pretty big details to leave out. Abram heads out anyway.

He figures God will find a way around the impossibilities. And what is the result? His life gets worse. He is seventy-five when he starts out on this journey to the unknown place to which God calls him, so he might at least expect God to act quickly. God doesn't. And he doesn't bother to make Abram and Sarai's life easy while they wait on him to fulfill his promises. They find famine in Canaan, which drives them to Egypt, which turns into a complicated mess that gets them kicked out of the country. After that, more years go by as Abram raises livestock, deals with disputes over flocks and herds, and takes care of business with his nephew

Lot. Still, there is no visible progress toward the fulfillment of the Big Promises of God.

Abram is stuck, in other words, just the way many of us have felt as we slog our way through our lives, hoping for answers from the Lord. More trouble follows. Lot is taken captive, and Abram has to put together a small army and go to battle to rescue him. He succeeds, but might he wonder, *Is getting embroiled in this kind of conflict what my life is supposed to be about?* His life is slipping away; the years are passing. Where is God?

The Lord appears to Abram in another vision and promises "a very great reward." This time Abram speaks up. He says, "You have given me no children; so a servant in my household will be my heir" (Genesis 15:3). It's hard not to feel Abram's disappointment in this scene. He has been waiting a long time. He has suffered. He has heard these promises before. The fulfillment of them seems even more impossible now than it did ten years earlier.

In response, God doesn't explain what is taking so long, nor does he offer a timeline for the future, nor does he tell exactly how he is going to fulfill his seemingly impossible promise. He simply reassures Abram that the promised heir will be Abram's own flesh and blood, not a servant of his household. And he tells him to look up in the sky and count the stars. "So shall your offspring be," God says (Genesis 15:5).

Sounds improbable, at best.

The Lord makes a covenant with Abram, who keeps believing. But *when* will it be fulfilled? And *how?* This couple is old. They don't have time to wait. Sarai comes up with a plan to move things along. Since she isn't giving birth, she offers her servant, Hagar, as a surrogate to have the child with Abram. He does have a child with Hagar—Ishmael—but the situation does not turn out well. Conflict erupts between Hagar and Sarai. Ishmael is not the fulfillment of God's promise. More years of waiting and confusion lie ahead. Abram is eighty-six years old on the day Ishmael is born. How much more can he or Sarai stand? How much more could any of us endure?

Thirteen more years go by before any real, new progress is made. It's so easy to say it—thirteen years. But how much agony does that length of time represent? Now Abram is ninety-nine; Sarai is ninety. It's as if God wants to ratchet up the Impossibility Level as high as he can before he steps in to act.

Finally Sarai—now called Sarah—gives birth to Isaac. It is not an easy year; it includes the destruction of nearby Sodom and Gomorrah and other difficulties, but the long-promised baby finally arrives when Abraham is one hundred years old. God has accomplished the impossible.

Now That One Impossibility Is Resolved, How About Another?

By now, after all those years of turmoil, the God-favored Abraham will surely be allowed to live out his life in ease and peace, right? He has more than paid his dues. He is past one hundred. He has believed and trusted God's promises. Shouldn't he be allowed to settle comfortably into raising Isaac for whatever years he has left then die peacefully, knowing that God's promise for his offspring is safely on track?

Instead, God confronts Abraham with another test of embracing the impossible. If waiting for a son for all those tumultuous decades was hard, this newest test will be far worse, stretching anyone's ability to keep believing that God really has Abraham's best interests at heart and intends to keep his promises.

God tells Abraham to sacrifice Isaac.

The audacity of this command, the outrage of it, the seeming cruelty, are astonishing. Think of it. This long-awaited son—the miracle of Abraham and Sarah's old age, the hope of their future, the center of their very purpose in God's story—is to be killed, not by accident or illness, but on purpose, by the command of God? This horrifying deed is to be carried out not by an assassin, not by a political enemy, but by his own father, who treasures him more than anyone else on earth.

Nothing up to now in Abraham's story shows his complete, blind faith in God as does his willingness to carry out this command. It's too bad this story is already so familiar to many of us. Many of us have heard it so many times that we can't even remember a time when we didn't know how it turns out. If you already know, try again to see it fresh. Watch it unfold in Genesis 22. After God orders Abraham to take his beloved son and offer him as a burnt offering on the mountain God will lead him to, I wish everyone reading the story would have to stop and contemplate this command for the same length of time that Abraham does. Abraham does not know the end of the story. What must he be thinking as he saddles his donkey and splits the wood for the offering then travels with Isaac and his two servants for *three days* to the place of sacrifice? Scripture records nothing of Abraham's thoughts. It records only his obedience. We have to fill in the agony for ourselves.

Most of us could not force ourselves even to begin that journey. We would say no to the Lord even before we gather the first piece of wood or pull out the saddle for the donkey. We would feel betrayed by God that God would even suggest such a thing. After all those years of waiting for this son? After all the confusion, the hassles, the battles, the family strife? Is this really how the story ends? This is what God is like? Many of us would turn our backs on God at that moment, and we would feel justified in doing so. We would live out our lives in bitter disappointment with the Lord.

Some might go along with the plan for a while, knowing there would still be time to turn back eventually. There would be time to bargain with God, to show God how wrong this is, before it is too late. Some might make that entire, agonizing, three-day trip up the mountain, hoping for some clarification from God or some outside force—an earthquake, a flood, anything—to counteract God's command and take the decision out of their hands.

Abraham goes all the way. He rides up the mountain with Isaac, he takes the wood for the offering, which he has cut himself, and he makes Isaac carry it to the place where the sacrifice will take place. Abraham carries the knife and the flint for fire. He builds the altar on which he will kill his still unsuspecting son. How can he do it? How can he contemplate it? Kill not just his son but the future of his people, everything he has lived for?

Abraham embraces the impossible. He is carrying the knife and the flint to make the fire. He builds the altar. When Isaac asks where the sheep is for the burnt offering, Abraham still does not waver from his trust in the Lord. He answers that God will provide the lamb for the offering. If God is going to put a stop to this outrageous act, isn't now the time?

Abraham keeps going. He places the wood on his altar, binds Isaac and places him on top of it. He takes the cleaver and reaches out to slaughter his son.

How many times over those three days has Abraham imagined this moment? Does he really think he will be able to slice into his own son with this knife? Will God provide him the will to do it? How much thought has Abraham given to what will happen after Isaac's death? How will he explain it to the servants who are with him? What will he tell Sarah? How can life go on after such a deed?

At the last second, God calls out and tells Abraham not to kill Isaac. Abraham has passed the test of faith. He looks up and sees a ram to offer instead. God says through an angel,

I swear by myself, declares the LORD, that because you have done this and have not withheld your son, your only son, I will surely bless you and make your descendants as numerous as the stars in the sky and as the sand on the seashore. Your descendants will take possession of the cities of their enemies, and through your offspring all nations on earth will be blessed, because you have obeyed me. (Genesis 22:16-18)

An Act of Faith that Still Echoes Today

Abraham cannot even know all the ways in which his suffering and frustration and obedience to God's inscrutable commands—not only in this incident but in all the years leading up to it—will be redeemed throughout the coming centuries. He cannot know the full implications of God's promise that his offspring will bless the world.

Abraham cannot imagine how his own story will parallel a much larger story—the sacrifice of Jesus Christ on the cross. In both stories, a father shows his willingness to sacrifice his beloved son. In both stories the son climbs a hill as he carries the wood that will be instrumental in his own slaughter. Both Isaac and Jesus are bound to that wood in preparation for their killing. Both appear to be willing to give their lives to achieve the will of their fathers. Jesus certainly goes willingly, and Scripture records no struggle on Isaac's part against the horrible fate he barely escapes. In both cases the courageous willingness to suffer an excruciating death leads to indescribable blessings for others that extend for centuries beyond the incident itself—in fact, they extend into eternity.

The implications of these deeds are not clear to everyone at the time they occur. Can Isaac fully know what this bizarre episode is all about? How about the two servants who accompany him and Abraham on this trip? How about Sarah when she finds out? Jesus's disciples do not understand the implications of his crucifixion. Not until after his resurrection do they begin to make sense of it.

How similar this is to the stories of suffering Christians that I have been following throughout these chapters. None of them knew the reasons for their adversity, nor could they foresee the unusual and sometimes dramatic ways that God would redeem it. They simply walked through it, as Abraham did, and only later did they begin to see hints that their pain has not been wasted. Sometimes hints are *all* they get in this lifetime because, like Abraham and Isaac, most of the ways in which God will make use of their stories won't happen until long after they are gone from this earth.

When I see situations that look impossible to redeem, I think of Abraham and Isaac. Like Abraham, I *choose* to believe in a redemption I not only cannot see but cannot even *imagine*. Even when a situation is so complex and seemingly so beyond saving that I don't even know what outcome to ask for, I take my stand as a believer in the God of the impossible. When Abraham stands poised with a knife only inches away from his tied-up son, that choice of faith is all he has. He stakes everything on his trust in God. And it saves him.

Go to beaconhillbooks.com/go/nothingiswasted for a free downloadable study guide that includes questions for deeper personal reflection as well as activities for use in a small group setting.

5 ⁓ THE GOD
WHO THWARTS

"I was hit by a car once while crossing the street, and it was the best thing that ever happened to me."

Amie Longmire tossed out that provocative statement in the middle of a speech that was about a different topic entirely. She didn't explain. She said she didn't have time to get into it. She let the idea dangle there as she finished her prepared remarks.

I couldn't let that go. I had to know how getting hit by a car could possibly have been the best thing that ever happened to her. I didn't know her, but after the meeting I contacted her to see if she would tell me the rest of the story. She was happy to tell it. The accident had taken place four years earlier, when she worked as a guidance counselor in the psychology department at a seminary in a busy downtown area. It was a day in October when she had a particularly heavy workload.

"It was a bad day to get hit by a car," she said. As she stepped out into the street at a busy intersection, she was hit by a car whose driver was trying to make a left turn on a yellow light. "I saw too late the grill of her car."

Amie was knocked so hard that she flipped a few times in the air—three, she thinks—fell on the hood of the car, and then landed about fifteen feet away. She was so afraid of being run over again by the car—she didn't know whether it had stopped—that she popped back up immediately. Two women who saw the accident came over and urged her to lie back down.

By the time the ambulance and police came, Amie was freezing and in shock. She was transported to the hospital but had to stay there for only about six hours. Amazingly, nothing was broken, and she had never lost consciousness. The doctor told her, "Normally people die when they hit their head like that."

People kept telling Amie how "lucky" she was, but she didn't feel lucky—she had been hit by a car! Although she had come through the accident better than expected, she still had some serious injuries. She had a concussion, bad road rash on her left hip and left arm, and she couldn't move her shoulder.

The aftermath of the accident was not easy either. She went back to work the next day but started physical therapy through worker's compensation, which ended up being slow and complicated. The legal case that emerged from the accident was difficult to settle and took more than two years. She ended up having three MRIs, eight sets of X-rays, two physical therapists, and two orthopedists. Her hip still bothers her, more than five years after the accident. Her neurologist also told her she had post-concussion syndrome, similar to what some injured football players get, with forgetfulness and sensitivity to light and noise. She had a headache for six months. Even now, when she teaches, she has trouble remembering names.

Amie's story is one of the best examples I have seen of a type of redemption I believe God sometimes uses to get us where he wants us to be. Instead of always *fulfilling* our desires, as we hope he will do, God sometimes *thwarts* them as an act of love to divert us onto a better path. Do I believe he caused the car to hit Amie? No. But I do believe he used it as an opportunity to allow Amie to rethink the direction her life was going. Amie thinks so too.

Amie says the accident, painful and inconvenient though it was, got her "unstuck." She realized she had settled into a rut doing work she didn't really want to do. The accident was a wake-up call that showed her that if she could survive getting hit by a car, then she had "permission to take some risks."

The transformation in her thinking began right away, even as the paramedic was taking her away from the scene. As he treated her and asked about her job, he asked her whether she'd gone to school for this kind of work and whether it was really what she wanted to do.

She answered no, it wasn't what she really wanted to do.

"What would you do if you could do what you really wanted?" he asked.

She immediately knew that what she wanted to do was go to graduate school to study writing.

That was October. By December she had applied for a master's degree program in writing at a nearby university. She was accepted and started the program in January. She said her attitude was, "Okay, I'm alive. I'll do this thing." She was unstuck and headed down a path that was far more meaningful to her than her other career.

She pursued her master's degree and continued in her old job for eight more months until she was offered a teaching fellowship at the university where she studied. She finished her master's in professional writing a couple years later and now teaches writing at a university, writes magazine articles, and is turning her thesis into a book.

Before this experience, Amie had thought of the pursuit of a career in writing as a far-off, scary thing to do. She had carefully stayed on the safer path. It's hard to miss the symbolism of what happened to her. She was literally knocked off a road. The physical road she had chosen, like the road of life on which she felt stuck, turned out to be the wrong one, but it took some creative thwarting to move her to the right one.

When God Knocks You Down

Dramatic, thwarted journeys have a long history among Christians. One day a man named Saul, who recently stood by approvingly as a group of men stoned to death a Christian named Stephen, is making his way down a road toward the synagogues in Damascus, where he hopes to find more Christians to take prisoner and haul back to Jerusalem. Described as a man who is "still breathing out murderous threats against the Lord's disciples" (Acts 9:1), Saul is not a man for whom subtle hints or gentle prodding seem to work. If God is going to reach him, the message will have to be bold. Saul will need to be thwarted in a way he cannot ignore.

God confronts Saul in just such a dramatic way. As Saul and his traveling companions hurry down that road, eager to torment Christians, a light from heaven flashes around him. The shock of it knocks him down. That gets his attention.

Then he hears a voice say, "Saul, Saul, why do you persecute me?" (Acts 9:4). Saul asks who is speaking, and the voice answers, "I am Jesus, whom you are persecuting" (Acts 9:5). Jesus then tells him to go into the city, where he will be told what to do. As if all this were not traumatic enough, Saul is also stricken with temporary blindness. He doesn't eat or drink anything for three days. He has to be led by the hand to Damascus, where he waits for whatever will happen next. He is weak and blind. The entire course of his life has been changed forever because of this drastically thwarted trip.

I have often envied Saul's conversion story. I love the clarity of it. Jesus swoops down in a blaze of light, knocks Saul down, and says, "Stop persecuting me!" That is a huge contrast to the spiritual lives of so many of us, where the choices seem murky and it's difficult to figure out exactly where God fits into our story and exactly what he wants us to do. Why doesn't God reveal himself in these blinding-light interventions more often?

On the other hand, maybe he does it more often than we think. Maybe we simply don't recognize the thwarting intervention in the form in which it arrives. Take Amie Longmire's accident as an example. She didn't see a blazing light or hear the voice of God when the car ran into her, but could the message for her life have been any clearer even if those elements had been part of the mishap? *I was hit by a car once, and it was the best thing that ever happened to me.* The way this accident was going to shake her out of her complacency and put her on a different path was clear to her even before they loaded her into the ambulance. Could a blazing light from heaven have worked any faster? Even Saul has to wait three days in blindness and without food in order to figure out the direction God is calling him to go. For Amie, the change was immediate.

The problem with the way most of our lives get thwarted is that it often feels like failure rather than God's auspicious intervention. Who wants to get hit by a car? Who wants their plans suddenly upended? If God intervenes, we most often prefer that he simply do what we ask. We may think we want the blazing-light clarity he gives Saul, but usually what we really want is for God to do things our way.

When Failure Pushes Us to Where We Need to Be

My own story doesn't appear to have any Saul-like moments, but if I examine it carefully, I see that it is full of God's creative thwarting. Today I am grateful for the job I have as a professor at Azusa Pacific University. This place where I have worked for almost twenty-five years seems ideal for me now. I wouldn't have wanted to land anywhere else because of how well this position has worked out both personally and professionally. But in the year before I applied to teach here, I applied for a position at another university. I desperately wanted to go there. I prayed fervently that it would work out. I researched not only the university but the city and region where it was located. As I looked at photos of the place, I envisioned my life there. I could *taste* that job. It was mine. I was one of the finalists for the position. They *had* to offer it to me.

I didn't get the job. The disappointment clung to me like a huge weight, pulling me down. I pushed through the next few months feeling bogged down by almost every facet of life. I slogged through my dissertation, trying to finish graduate school after many years of work. I didn't know whether I really had the drive and skill to finish anymore. I felt stalled and restless in my current job. I wondered whether anything was going to work out the way I hoped, or whether stalled would become the theme of my life. I had been turned down for jobs before, but this rejection was harder to take because I had felt so confident that God was going to answer this prayer the way I wanted. Going to this place had felt so *right*. Why would God thwart this opportunity?

I kept working, and that fall I started applying for more jobs. I sent letters to thirty-four universities across the country. Some responded with letters of rejection. Some ignored me entirely. The chair of the English Department at Azusa Pacific University wrote to tell me they had no openings. I added his letter to the rejection pile and kept hoping.

No job offers came through, and by the spring of that school year, when the time came to decide whether I would sign my contract for the following year at the school where I was teaching, I had only one other possibility, a college in Ohio. I started to really want this job but not with the intensity I had felt for the one the year before. I was moving a little more cautiously now. I knew how quickly these possibilities could be yanked away.

I was chosen as one of the final two candidates for the college in Ohio. They brought the two of us to interview on the same day but tried to keep us apart as we did our teaching presentations and went through our series of interviews with department members and administrators. Still, I did pass the other candidate on the sidewalk for one brief, awkward moment, as his escorts led him in the opposite direction of where my hosts were taking me. I looked at him and wondered, *Does he want this job as much as I do? Who will end up disappointed at the end of this process?*

I felt good by the time I flew home after the interview. All the signals were in my favor. I was almost certain that the hints I was receiving indicated I was the top choice. I waited for the job offer.

I didn't get the job. They chose the other guy. Thwarted again. Not only was I disappointed, but other pressures were also pushing in on me. My dissertation deadline was only a few weeks away, and I still had lots of work to do. I was trying to keep up with a full load of classes at the busiest time of the semester. I also had to decide whether to sign the contract for another year at my current university, which meant giving up hope of being offered any of the other jobs I had applied for.

Then I got another call from Azusa Pacific University, the same school that, months earlier, had told me they had no openings. Now they did have one, and the English Department chair, whom I had met at a conference, called to see if I was still interested. With the deadline quickly approaching for signing the contract at the university where I was teaching, I awkwardly asked for an extension on the deadline and flew out to California for the interview.

This time I got the job, and I have worked for this university ever since. Even though I knew little about the school when

I first applied, I have loved my time here and have been well supported as a teacher and writer. APU feels like home. I can tell it is the right place. Would those other colleges have worked out well? They might have, but now I'm glad I came here instead. What once felt like God's blocking of my prayers now looks like his guidance into the place where he wanted me.

One benefit of getting hired at APU is that I met my wife here in southern California, something I never could have anticipated when I longed for the jobs at the other places. The fact that those openings were thwarted indirectly led me to Peggy, for whom I am very grateful. Might another wife have awaited in one of those other places? Possibly, but I believe Peggy and I were meant to be together.

I could list many other good things that sprang from the opportunity to move to California and work at APU—our kids were born here, we bought our home here, we have made good friends here, and we worship and serve in a good church. None of that would have happened, at least not here, with these people and these circumstances, without the thwarting of my earlier dream of working at that other university. At the time I felt only the crush of disappointment. Now I believe God had a better plan.

What About Thwarting that Appears to Serve No Purpose?

When I hear about Amie Longmire getting hit by the car, it's easy to see God's fingerprints on that thwarting of her usual routine, which pushed her toward her true calling. But does that mean that all the thwarting that she and the rest of us face serves such purpose? It seems dangerous to go that far. By all appearances, much of the thwarting people endure doesn't lead to a clear-cut, recognizable outcome that is better than if the thwarting had not happened. When, for example, a single mother has trouble finding a job she desperately needs to take care of her children, how could that thwarting possibly lead to anything good? When people train for years for a certain calling, taking on student loan debt and sacrificing uncounted hours to prepare for that field, and then they are shut out of that profession, what good can come of it? What if bad health thwarts a pastor from completing his life work, sidelining him instead?

I do not want to minimize the heartache and bewilderment that certain kinds of blocked opportunities can cause. In this life we may simply never know why we are so painfully thwarted in so many ways. Sometimes it is hard to see these things as anything but the result of evil. God has *sprinkled* redemption throughout various circumstances, but the world is not yet *bathed* in it. We await eternity for ultimate redemption, and in the meantime, we will suffer. As Romans 8:22 puts it, "We know that the whole creation has been groaning as in the pains of childbirth right up to the present time." The pain is sometimes so vivid that it blocks from our perception the hints of redemption in our lives. However, if you look carefully, you can often find those hints, and they can infuse your harsh circumstances with hope.

Just because a thwarting looks bad from a purely human perspective does not mean that it *is* bad from a spiritual perspective. One question to consider is, where does God want us? Where do we *need* to be in order to do the work he wants to do in us and in order for us to serve a purpose in the kingdom of God? That place may not be the one we would choose, and it may take a long time to see how being there could serve any purpose for anyone. Will we find the faith to trust God even when we can't make sense of his guidance?

Another way to look at this is, what unexpected bad consequences might there be if we were *never* thwarted and always got what we wanted? Think of your own past. Can you recall a relationship that, at the time, you would have given almost anything to have but now realize would have been destructive in the long run? Maybe you can think of a relationship that you *did* have that lasted for a while but that left you devastated when it ended. Can you now see ways in which you are better off that it ended? Can you think of some other passion of your younger years—for some experience, or achievement, or possession—that at the time felt as if it would be the fulfillment of all your desires but that now you see would not have satisfied you for all that long? Can you think of one of these passions that *was* fulfilled but that still eventually left you wanting more?

The longer ago these experiences occurred, the more likely it is that the thwarting you experienced will make sense and that you can see some good that came from it. That is not true in every case, of course. Some disappointments last a lifetime. And whenever we are in the middle of a disappointment, we certainly are not much comforted by the idea that the thwarting may one day be redeemed. We want what we want right now, and no explanation will lessen that desire while it burns within us. But if faith in God means anything, it means that even during a painful thwarting, we can at least hang on to our trust in his guidance of our lives even when his actions don't make sense to us.

Can you think of people who have almost never been thwarted, at least in any outward way? They appear to get whatever they want. Young and beautiful, they have the whole world laid out at their feet. Whatever fame, whatever wealth, whatever pleasure, whatever power they desire is lavished upon them. Is this lack of thwarting generally good for them? Does it lead to the kind of life that brings lasting contentment and spiritual health?

On just about any day, I can go to celebrity news sites and find multiple stories of the wrecked lives of young actors and singers who have almost never received the answer "no" to any desire, yet they have undermined their own success with bad behavior of various kinds. Although thousands of other people would kill for even a fraction of the opportunities for wealth and fame that have been afforded to these unhappy young stars, the un-thwarted celebrities who possess these gifts have often squandered them. It's easy to read these stories and judgmentally shake our heads in disapproval of these spoiled brats. If *we* were in their shoes, we tell ourselves, we would be different. We would know how to handle these privileges. We would not fall prey to the temptations of overindulgence, arrogance, pride, or addiction. We would stay spiritually centered *and* drink in all that power, money, pleasure, and fame. In fact, we would be enjoying some of those things already if so many forces of life had not thwarted us. It's not fair.

Is it possible that God, by thwarting some of our prayers or plans, is sparing us some of the pain that appears on those celebrity gossip sites or that is paraded on celebrity reality TV shows? Maybe you never sought such grandiose gifts from God in the first place. Maybe you sought only a humble job, or a quiet relationship, or an ordinary lifestyle, and even *those* desires were thwarted. How could any of those things possibly have led you astray? It's not as if you were trying to sell your soul for fame, or abandoning your principles in order to grasp wealth at any cost. Why would you be thwarted?

The truth is, we may not know where God wants us, either to make us the kind of people he wants us to be or to help someone else in ways we may only dimly understand. In the Bible, does it serve any purpose for Paul to be in prison repeatedly? For Moses to spend forty years working in the desert of Midian? For Joseph to be thrown into a pit? For Jeremiah to be thrown into a pit? For Stephen to be stoned? For Jonah to be swallowed by the fish? For Peter, Andrew, James, and John to be pulled away from careers as fishermen? For Matthew to give up his lucrative career as a tax collector? The answer is yes; all those unexpected deviations from the expected paths of these biblical figures serve significant purposes that still matter to us today. At the time, the people involved might prefer to stay out of the pit or the fish's belly, or they might feel more at ease continuing with the careers they have chosen. But God has bigger plans for them, which in most cases involve pain, difficulty, and sometimes even death. But those plans also involve eternal consequences.

If you read Paul's letters in the New Testament, you realize he has a tough time staying out of prison. He doesn't even seem to *try* that hard to stay out of jail. He certainly won't compromise his message in order to stay out of trouble. Arranging a life that is prosperous and smooth isn't a priority for Paul. He jumps into the fray and trusts God for whatever the outcome might be.

For Paul, the outcome is that he is killed for his faith. Leading up to that tragic end, his entire Christian life consists of one episode after another of thwarted plans, danger, and trouble. See how he describes it:

Five times I received from the Jews the forty lashes minus one. Three times I was beaten with rods, once I was pelted with stones, three times I was shipwrecked, I spent a night and a day in the open sea, I have been constantly on the move. I have been in danger from rivers, in danger from bandits, in danger from my fellow Jews, in danger from Gentiles; in danger in the city, in danger in the country, in danger at sea; and in danger from false believers. I have labored and toiled and have often gone without sleep; I have known hunger and thirst and have often gone without food; I have been cold and naked. (2 Corinthians 11:24-27)

Does Paul consider these endless thwartings failures? Does he believe God has let him down? On the contrary, Paul treats each diversion from his Plan A as an opportunity to serve God where he is. I can't claim that I treat my own times of being thwarted with the grace or maturity that Paul does, but I am trying to learn from him. He simply does not tie his mission or his contentment to circumstances that are beyond his control. When he is free, he pursues his mission vigorously. When he is in prison, he does what he can there (including writing a big chunk of the New Testament).

In fact, Paul has so perfected the art of adjusting to the diversions life throws his way that when he writes Philippians (in prison), he is able to say that he has "learned to be content whatever the circumstances. I know what it is to be in need, and I know what it is to have plenty. I have learned the secret of being content in any and every situation, whether well fed or hungry, whether living in plenty or in want" (Philippians 4:11-12). When a person writes that while literally chained up in jail, it has strong credibility.

It would be easy for someone in Paul's situation to turn bitter toward God for allowing him to be thrown in prison rather than remaining free to do the work God has called him to do. But early in his letter, Paul says that the gospel has actually been *advanced* because of his imprisonment. He says that "it has become clear throughout the whole palace guard and to everyone else that I am in chains for Christ. And because of my chains, most of the brothers and sisters have become confident in the Lord and dare all the more to proclaim the gospel without fear" (Philippians 1:13-14).

Paul allows no circumstance, whether good or bad, to be wasted. If God allows him to be somewhere, he assumes God must have some purpose for him there. Such flexibility and such an eternal view of what is significant are not easy to maintain, but, as Paul teaches in Philippians, they are the key to contentment.

Go to beaconhillbooks.com/go/nothingiswasted for a free downloadable study guide that includes questions for deeper personal reflection as well as activities for use in a small group setting.

6 ⁓ WHY WE LIKE STORIES ABOUT TROUBLE

Why do people spend so much time and money watching movies? Why do they spend hours turning page after page of novels? Why do they play video games in which they pretend to be people in the worst kinds of danger?

Entertainment? Escape?

Or is there a deeper reason?

Think of how much of your life you spend in the alternative universe of stories—either telling, hearing, watching, playing, or reading. We tell stories at the dinner table, at coffee shops, on the phone, at work, on airplanes, in waiting rooms. We read stories on the internet, hear them on the radio, watch them in movie theaters, hear them in sermons, read them in Scripture, play them in video games, and devour them in novels. We pay billions of dollars to the moviemakers, novelists, and video game creators who will tell us good stories.

Why is the thirst for story never quenched? If we see a good movie, we don't think, *Oh, that was enjoyable. Now I can move on to other things and don't need any more movies.* If we read a good novel, we don't think, *That was good. Now I'm done with that novelist.* Instead, we're more likely to want to watch *another* movie by that director or read *another* book by that author. From the time we are small children until the day we die, humans long for stories. Why?

Why We Go Looking for Trouble

One person who has devoted himself to studying our obsession with stories is Jonathan Gottschall, author of *The Storytelling Animal: How Stories Make Us Human*. He rejects the idea that our love of stories is mainly about escape, even though that is the most common explanation people give him. He writes, "If the escapist theory were true, we'd expect stories to be mainly about pleasurable wish fulfillment. In story worlds, everything would go right and good people would never suffer."[1]

In our real lives, we would love such a scenario, but in a movie or novel, we would never stand for something so dull. Fictional stories contain a paradox. As Gottschall puts it, "We are drawn to fiction because fiction gives us pleasure. But most of what is actually in fiction is deeply unpleasant: threat, death, despair, anxiety, Sturm und Drang."[2]

What do we want in our novels and movies and TV shows? We want trouble.

This deep desire for conflict in stories is true of people at any age, even small children. As Gottschall points out, even nursery rhymes are stories in which "babies fall out of trees 'cradle and all,' a little boy mutilates a dog, an old woman who lives in a shoe cruelly whips her starving children, blind mice are hacked up with carving knives, Cock Robin is murdered, and Jack smashes his skull."[3]

Stories that children make up themselves are no less filled with turmoil and violence. Here, for example, is a story made up by a three-year-old boy for his teacher: "The monkeys, they went up sky. They fall down. Choo choo train in the sky. I fell down in the sky in the water. I got on my boat and my legs hurt. Daddy fall down from the sky."[4]

But doesn't life contain enough trouble without the need for us to go looking for it—and even *paying* for it—in the stories that entertain us?

As a literature professor, I make a living teaching stories. Readers love them for many reasons—the excitement, the suspense, the joy of entering into the lives of other people and *becoming* those characters for a time. Those are reasons people are aware of. But I suspect there are also other forces that lure us toward stories.

Throughout our lives we are gripped by a few inescapable fears and desires. We sense that, regardless of how things appear on the surface of our lives, we are in trouble, and we are drawn to stories that show us what to do about it. What will save us? Who will rescue us? How will we respond if the worst thing happens?

Christianity teaches that, because of sin, the whole world is in deep trouble. We need a Savior. We cannot save ourselves on our own. Unfortunately, many of us live in denial of that dilemma. We convince ourselves we are *not* in trouble. Or, even if we are, Jesus Christ is not the answer. But through our love and obsession with stories—and through the very *existence* of stories—God may be planting within us hints of our need and longing for redemption. At a level deeper than we are often consciously aware, perhaps we like trouble in stories because we sense it in ourselves, and we are searching for a way out.

Jonathan Gottschall, who is not writing from a Christian perspective, gives this master formula for the kinds of fictional stories that people are drawn to:

Story = Character + Predicament + Attempted Extrication[5]

That pattern, which is universal but which Gottschall calls "intensely strange," considering the many other ways stories could be structured, follows a structure of redemption. Like so many other elements of life, that pattern points toward the ultimate redemption in Jesus Christ. Christian redemption happens when a character (me) faces the predicament (sin and separation from God) and pursues attempted extrication (salvation through Jesus Christ). One reason this pattern is so persistent is that the smaller redemptions in the stories we enjoy foreshadow the ultimate redemption in Christ that we crave, even if we are not aware of that craving.

The urge toward redemption in stories is so strong that we are often willing to overlook certain flaws or absurdities in a story if that redemptive pattern is brought to life in a satisfying way. One of the best examples of that is a story most of us have known since childhood, the story of Cinderella.

Why We Don't Mind the Absurdities in Cinderella

Novelists know that readers can be picky when it comes to getting the details of a story right. Readers are quick to pick up on even the slightest errors of fact or inconsistencies in a story. In a realistic novel, for example, if the novelist describes a certain building or landmark as being on the north side of the street when in fact it is on the south side of the street, plenty of finger-wagging readers are almost certain to fire off emails and letters of protest.

However, some classic stories get away with much bigger absurdities that readers either don't notice or don't mind. *Cinderella* is a story that has been told in dozens of versions over many centuries. There is a Chinese version, a German version, a Disney version, and many others. I teach the story in one of my literature courses, and our university library has more than fifty versions of the story, including a Korean Cinderella, a Persian Cinderella, a Western Cinderella (called Cindy Ellen), a Cajun Cinderella (called Cendrillon), a male Cinderella (called Prince Cinders), and many others. Many film versions of the story have been made, including a musical, the Disney cartoon, and newer versions, such as *A Cinderella Story*, that put the Cinderella-like girl in a modern setting.

The deep appeal of this story is undeniable, but *why* is it so universally popular? It contains implausible elements that readers should object to, but they don't. Take the Disney-animated version of the 1950s and the Brothers Grimm version, which are two of the most well-known adaptations of the story. When I speak of implausible elements, I am not referring to the fantasy details—a fairy godmother, a pumpkin that turns into a carriage, talking mice, and so on. Those make sense within the fantasy genre. The implausible elements I am talking about are things that defy logic and common sense even within the fairy tale genre. So accept, for a moment, the pumpkin coach and the mice who become footmen and the impractical glass slippers and the whole idea of love at first sight between Cinderella and the prince. Without elements like that, you wouldn't have a fairy tale. But how much sense do the following details make?

• The prince dances with Cinderella at the ball for hours (in some versions of the story, he even dances with her on multiple consecutive evenings), and he falls in love with her, and he even wants to marry her, yet he doesn't bother to nail down even the basics of her identity, such as her name, where she lives, or anything about her background?

• Her stepmother and stepsisters don't recognize her at the ball simply because she is dressed up?

• The prince takes the glass slipper around to every girl in the kingdom yet can't recognize the love of his life simply by *looking at her face*, which he gazed at longingly for hours during the dance? Simply because she is no longer wearing her fancy clothes? Or he doesn't know simply by *talking* to her?

- Craziest of all, the prince believes a shoe will fit *only one woman*?

His methods seems about the worst way to go about finding this girl, but readers don't care. Some versions of the Cinderella story try to make the elements a little more plausible, but some are even worse. In the Brothers Grimm version, for example, one of the stepsisters cuts off her toes in order to fit into the shoes, and *the prince doesn't notice* until they are far down the road and the blood starts pouring out. Even then, a bird has to alert him to the blood! Then the other sister tries the same trick, only she cuts off her heels instead, but the dim-witted prince, who you might think would be suspicious of such tricks by now, gets fooled again until the (much smarter) bird again points out the blood.

This story shouldn't work. Readers should rebel. When it comes to *Cinderella*, where are all those picky readers who howl at a misspelled word or missing apostrophe, or who bellow when a character with brown eyes is later mistakenly said to have blue eyes?

My purpose is not to denigrate *Cinderella*. I love it too. When I am not in such an analytical mode, I simply sit back and enjoy the story like everyone else. But why do readers love it? I believe they are willing to overlook the implausibilies in the story because the story itself strikes at a deep longing—the innate desire for redemption. I don't think readers are consciously aware of the idea of redemption as they read or watch *Cinderella*, any more than they pay attention to the story's absurdities. The story operates at a deeper level; otherwise, it wouldn't work.

But consider this. Whenever you read or watch *Cinderella*, with whom do you identify? For almost every reader, the answer is Cinderella. That is true whether you're male or female, or whether your actual life experience is closer to one of the other characters. Even if you're a father who has a daughter, as I am, you still become Cinderella as you read this story. Even if you're a stepmother, evil or not, you put yourself in Cinderella's shoes (so to speak). When you do that, what are you responding to?

Cinderella is in a terrible predicament. She is trapped by forces beyond her control. She sees no way out. Who can rescue her? Who has the power and the will to remove her from her misery? Only one person, the son of the king. She has no reason at the beginning of the story to believe that he would favor her or be willing to sacrifice anything for her. She has no reason to think he would even become aware of her. Yet, through the circumstances of the story, he does become aware of her. He does want to save her. As he searches for her, he shows that he will do anything to reach her, no matter how people try to thwart him, no matter how extravagant or bizarre his methods and sacrifices seem.

Doesn't that mirror the Christian story of redemption? The Son of God who loves you so much that no sacrifice, no matter how extreme, is too much? Is the crucifixion of Jesus extravagant? Of course. Bizarre? Yes. Am I complaining? No because, by it, we are saved.

The Greater the Loss, the More Powerful the Redemption

The redemptive pattern may be clear in a fairy tale like *Cinderella*, but do grittier, more disturbing stories also embody redemption? When I look at the works I teach in my college courses that focus on American literature from about two hundred years ago to the present, I see the pattern everywhere. One literary scholar, Christian R. Davis, goes so far as to say that the redemptive pattern is crucial to a story that truly connects with audiences. He says that the more closely the plot of a story follows "the Christian pattern of innocent and intentional sacrifice to bring salvation, the more powerfully readers tend to respond to the work of literature. In other words, the greater the danger or loss and the greater the sacrifice to redeem it, the more popular and/or emotionally powerful the literature will be."[6] In his book *Reading for Redemption*, Davis analyzes many examples of works that follow this redemptive pattern, such as the *Harry Potter* books, *A Tale of Two Cities*, *Ben-Hur*, *The Lord of the Rings*, *The Iliad*, *Hamlet*, *Oedipus*, and others.

When I look at the literary works that affect my students most deeply, I have to agree that the redemptive pattern is an important aspect of what makes a work successful, even if redemption is not an obvious element in the story. Often these works are written by authors who do not have any Christian purpose in mind and may even be hostile to Christianity. One example is Mark Twain's *The Adventures of Huckleberry Finn*. Students love this American classic, set in the 1830s. For both Huck and his friend, the escaped slave Jim, the plot of the story follows the redemptive pattern, both in the more general sense that Gottschall describes and also in the more specifically Christian sense as Davis defines it.

In terms of Gottschall's pattern, Huck's predicament is that his abusive father has held him captive in a cabin from which Huck extricates himself by faking his own murder. Then he goes on the run, fleeing not only his father but other constraints of "sivilization" that bother him. He soon runs into the character Jim, who has escaped from his owner, Miss Watson. Jim's predicament is that he most likely will be caught and severely punished for his escape. The extrication Jim seeks is to make it to a free state and out of the danger of slavery.

The novel is not overtly Christian. In fact, Twain pokes fun at Christianity throughout the book. Twain himself became increasingly bitter toward the Christian faith as time went on. Nevertheless, the novel fits the redemptive Christian pattern Davis describes, which is a work in which "a more-or-less Christlike redeemer risks or gives his or her life to redeem someone who is in danger of being lost."[7]

Huck, although baffled by Christianity in many ways, becomes a self-sacrificing redeemer for Jim. Huck has nothing personally to gain from helping an escaped slave. By doing so, Huck is only putting himself at risk, not to mention making his own journey more difficult. According to the corrupt values of his society, Huck should simply turn Jim over to the authorities and be finished with him. All his life Huck has been taught that slaves are mere property. By helping Jim, he is stealing from Jim's owner, Miss Watson.

Huck struggles with his decision of what to do about Jim. Although the reader cheers on Huck as he stands up for his friend, Huck is a naïve young teenager who believes that his conscience demands that he repent of this behavior. In one climactic scene, Huck actually writes a letter to Miss Watson, telling her where Jim is. As he finishes the letter and holds it in his hand, he feels good about writing it at first, but then he remembers all that he and Jim have gone through together and all that Jim has done for him. Trembling, he wavers about whether he can really do the so-called right thing and therefore betray his friend. Finally, he tears up the note and declares, "All right, then, I'll *go* to hell!"[8] Huck is willing to make any sacrifice, even facing the threat of hell, to save Jim.

In the process of helping Jim, Huck also finds him to be a true friend who helps Huck achieve his own freedom. At the end of the novel, Huck "lights out for the Territory," ready to start a new life. Although this novel has been controversial over the years for literary and racial reasons, readers continue to respond to the deep, redemptive friendship at the core of the book.

Why Would We Want to Read a Story that Ends Tragically?

Gottschall's pattern describes an attempted extrication from the character's predicament, and the word *attempted* is crucial. Not all stories end happily. But that does not mean they don't include redemption. One reason we are so drawn to stories in whatever form we consume them—novels, plays, short stories, video games, films, etc.—is that we are able to put ourselves in the main character's place and imagine how we would feel and what we would do if we were living that person's life. As we experience the story, we temporarily *become* the person in a sense, sometimes identifying with him or her so closely that we are brought to tears or experience the same fear, anger, or other emotion that the character feels. How many times have you sat in a movie and willed the character to make a different choice? Some people get so caught up in that identification that they shout out, "Don't go in there!" or, "Look out!" Even if a story turns out badly for a character, it can turn out well for us as readers or viewers as we ask ourselves questions such as, *What would I have done in that predicament? What other outcome was possible? What might have saved that character?*

My favorite play is Arthur Miller's *Death of a Salesman*. I teach it every chance I get, and I have read it and seen it onstage and onscreen more times than I can count. The main character in the play, Willy Loman, is a failure. He is getting old, losing his grip on reality, and is haunted by the past. His grown sons have disappointed him, especially Biff, his favorite, who showed so much promise as a high school football hero but who has failed to accomplish much of anything since then.

To Willy, there is no chance for redemption in his own story. As the title of the play indicates, he ends in destruction. The reader (or theatergoer), however, *does* see a way out for Willy. Failure and destruction are *not* inevitable.

The play alternates between the past and the present, and the viewer sees ways out for Willy in both time periods. In the past, he could choose a career more suited to his personality and skills than sales. He could raise his sons with different values. He could live with more personal integrity.

In the present, even though he loses his job and feels like everything he cares about is slipping away, he still has options. His family loves him. His friend Charley offers him a job. He has skills, such as carpentry and construction, that he could use to make a living. His life does not have to be wasted.

As with many tragic heroes, pride prevents Willy Loman from taking the steps necessary to avoid his downfall. Redemption is available to him, but he rejects it. He is too proud to set aside his rivalry with Charley and accept a job from him. He is too proud to work a manual labor job instead of making a living in the sales profession he has so misguidedly exalted. He has plenty of people trying to point the way out of his predicament. Charley, Willy's wife, Linda, and his son Biff all try to get Willy to face reality and take a path that will save him. Willy resolutely sticks to his tragic course and is destroyed.

Redemption, whether in the literary realm or the spiritual, is a choice. Readers and theatergoers who experience Willy Loman's story keep rooting for him to choose a way out of his predicament, but he doesn't. They see his path to redemption. He is blind to it.

Death of a Salesman highlights redemption in one other powerful way. Though his plan is misguided, Willy's purpose in wanting to kill himself is to offer new life—or redemption—to his failed son, Biff. Willy believes his own death would provide Biff an insurance settlement that would pave the way toward the young man's success. The reader, by seeing Willy's flawed choices, becomes aware of the choices that truly would have led Willy out of his predicament. The truth of redemption is made plain by Willy's stark rejection of it.

You don't even have to go to classic literature in order to see how much we seek redemption in stories of death and devastation. Simply go to your local movie theater. Or turn on your television or computer and scroll through the movie choices. It won't be long before you find one—or ten or fifteen—in which the world itself is at risk of destruction. How many movies can you list right now that follow some form of this very familiar apocalyptic theme and structure: The entire world (or maybe just the United States, or perhaps the White House) faces annihilation as the result of some overwhelming outside force such as aliens, or terrorists, or some horrible plague. Escape from this catastrophe appears impossible. Thousands or even millions may have already died, and it's only a matter of time before the rest of humanity, or the country, goes with it. Only one person (such as a Will Smith, Tom Cruise, Chris Hemsworth, etc.) can rescue everyone, but that person is an outsider or nonconformist in some way, and the establishment does not take him seriously as a rescuer at first. Many people may die before the hero emerges, ready to risk his own life to save everyone else's. He must fight a gigantic battle that requires all his courage and that looks unlikely to succeed, but ultimately he defeats the forces of evil.

Sound familiar? Does that bring half a dozen or so movies to mind? Why, in an age when actual terrorist atrocities and wars and other catastrophes already fill the news every day, do we choose to spend our entertainment dollars watching movies that depict something just as bad or even worse?

In the summer of 2013, *Christianity Today* reported on several movies released that summer that depicted the end of the world. One that fits the pattern I just described is *World War Z*, a film in which people all over the world have been infected with a mysterious virus that turns them into zombie-like creatures who alternately lash out violently or stand around in a stupor. Human life on earth is in danger of being swept away by this threat, and no one knows how to stop it. The world needs a rescuer. A character played by Brad Pitt—loving family man, regular guy, rugged hero—steps up at ultimate risk to himself in order to set things right.

Although movies like that are staples of every summer season, the *Christianity Today* writer Alissa Wilkinson noticed something different about many of the movies and TV shows released that year. While plenty followed the usual, generic, end-of-the-world pattern, a number of films and other shows went beyond zombies or terrorists to make specific references to biblical prophecy, especially in the book of Revelation.

Although these filmmakers and TV writers treated their subject matter with varying degrees of reverence or irreverence, something about that biblical apocalyptic vision must strike a deep chord in audiences, even though neither writers nor viewers may be approaching the shows as Christians. Wilkinson mentions a film called *Rapture-Palooza*, a comedy about "two star-crossed teenage lovers whose romance is blooming amid the events foretold in Revelation, who must also defeat the antichrist."[9] Then there is *This Is the End*, a present-day comedy in which a housewarming party turns into an end-of-the-world gathering for a group of friends as events from the book of Revelation take place outside. The TV show *Supernatural* depicts the bowl judgments from Revelation. A film called *The World's End* follows a group of friends who, during a night of drinking, find themselves facing the apocalypse.

Wilkinson doesn't even mention a number of other movies from the same year that also feature similar apocalyptic, dystopian themes. *Star Trek into Darkness*, for instance, tears up San Francisco, while *Man of Steel* serves up the annihilation of New York. *Elysium, After Earth,* and *Pacific Rim* pelt audiences with their own versions of these catastrophic themes.

Why so much apocalypse? Perhaps one reason is that, deep down, whether the audience members are Christians or not, they sense that this fallen world really is headed toward an ultimate, eternal transformation. Maybe a part of them senses the truth in John's words: "Then I saw 'a new heaven and a new earth,' for the first heaven and the first earth had passed away..." (Revelation 21:1). Those who might have trouble believing or understanding biblical prophecy directly might nevertheless feel pulled toward the truth of the temporary nature of this world and the approach of eternity. They might sense, however vaguely, the need for a Savior as that future unfolds.

If these apocalyptic movies were *only* about destruction—if they were merely vehicles that gave filmmakers an excuse to create cool special effects depicting loud, terrifying explosions wiping out skyscrapers and national monuments—then we could dismiss them as nothing more than popcorn movies offering a couple hours of exciting but rather mindless entertainment. In most of these films, however, destruction is not the final word.

Usually, the world is saved. Someone, the hero, often a kind of Christ figure, saves the world, or at least what is left of it, at the last minute. I have already mentioned the main character in *World War Z*, who fits such a Christ figure role, and I could mention dozens of other examples from these kinds of movies. Will Smith has played such a role in so many films that one writer analyzes Smith's recurring humanity-saving efforts in an article called "Will Smith Saves the World Again, and Again, and Again."[10] A different writer produced a chart that shows how many times Will Smith's characters saved all of humanity (nine), saved one or more people (six), or metaphorically saved one or more people (twice).[11] In the three *Men in Black* movies, for instance, Smith's character, along with his colleagues, saves the entire planet from aliens threatening Earth. In *Independence Day*, Smith's character also helps save America (except for a few cities that get destroyed) and the rest of the earth from the scourge of invading aliens. The list goes on as Smith saves the world, or at least a select group of nations and individuals, in films such as *I Am Legend*, *Hancock*, *After Earth*, and others.

Out of the horrible destruction that takes place in these films, hope for renewal, for peace, and for a better world often arises, just as the promise of "a new heaven and a new earth" redeems the destruction that occurs in Revelation. In the Bible, this bright eternity is possible because of Jesus's sacrifice. Those who enter this paradise do not do so because of their own worthiness. They do so only because Jesus's forgiveness has washed away their sins and made them right with God. In the apocalyptic films, the Christ-figure heroes who save so many people across the globe don't do so because those people have done anything to deserve it. The heroes believe those people as human beings are inherently worth saving. The heroes, like Jesus, are willing to die if necessary to secure that salvation. Like Jesus, these heroes, though self-sacrificing, are often rejected and misunderstood by the very people they are trying to save, especially those in leadership. Those heroes make the sacrifice anyway. Like Christ, they are shown as loving, tough, nonconformist, and courageous.

Some heroes in these kinds of movies follow the pattern of Christ's life in so many ways that the parallels are hard to ignore. Take the 2013 Superman movie, *Man of Steel*. The film has so many Christian elements that Warner Brothers prepared a resource ministry site for pastors to use, including sermon outlines, video clips, and images from the film to show in churches. In one outline for a small group session aimed at children, for example, the session leader is to compare Superman's mission to Jesus's mission with this statement: "In the movie, Superman first offers himself to save the earth. Superman loses, earth wins. But then he realizes he must *fight* to save the earth and *stay* to keep saving the earth. Christ didn't just give himself over to reverse the judgment against us, he did that then rose victorious—and continues to fight for us. These truths are reflected throughout the New Testament."[12] That leads to a discussion of John 3:16-17.

In *Man of Steel* the parallels to Christ are undeniable. The hero's father sends him to Earth and gives him earthly parents. He heals people and has other supernatural powers, although he grows up as a human and has to fight evil, Satan-like forces. At the age of thirty-three, he faces his biggest test, with huge stakes for saving humanity. Sound familiar?

Everywhere I Look, I See Jesus

When I look up at the bookshelves in my office, I see one example after another of novels that contain Christ figures and Christian imagery, even when those books are written by authors who reject Christianity itself. Take John Steinbeck's classic *The Grapes of Wrath*. Steinbeck was skeptical of Christianity, but among the many biblical references and symbols in his novel is a Christ figure, the ex-preacher Jim Casy. As many scholars have pointed out, Jim Casy has the same initials as Jesus Christ, he wanders the countryside with about as many Joads as Jesus had disciples, he prays and helps people, he courageously stands up to authorities, and he makes himself the ultimate sacrifice for others. As he confronts the men who want to kill him, he says, "You don' know what you're a-doin,'" a statement that echoes Christ's prayer for those who were about to crucify him: "Father, forgive them, for they do not know what they are doing" (Luke 23:34).[13]

A few books to the right of *The Grapes of Wrath* on my book-shelf sits Ernest Hemingway's masterpiece *The Old Man and the Sea*. Hemingway was certainly not enthusiastic about Christianity, but he still builds hints of Christ into his main character, Santiago. Like Christ struggling to carry his cross, the old man strains to carry his mast on his shoulder as he struggles up the road after his days-long ordeal with the fish. His battle also injures his hands in ways that are reminiscent of Christ's nail-pierced palms. As he lies down in his shack near the end of the novel, his position is similar to that of a man on a cross, with arms spread out and palms up.[14]

I could mention many other examples of Christ imagery in the American literature I teach. William Faulkner, a contemporary of Steinbeck and Hemingway, who also shared their skepticism toward Christianity, nevertheless built Christ imagery into his novels, including *The Sound and the Fury* and others. Stephen Crane includes it in *The Red Badge of Courage*, and the list could go on.

What is it about Jesus Christ that draws so many storytellers to include some version of him in their own stories, even when they are skeptical of him? Is it only because Jesus makes such a good and dramatic story? Or is there something deeper? Some might claim that the Christian story is merely one of countless stories that happen to follow the same redemptive pattern and that there is nothing special about the story of the life of Christ. We have Greek and Roman mythology, *Star Wars* mythology, Superman mythology, Christian mythology. If all these stories follow such similar patterns, then why should any of them be thought of as more important than the others?

What makes the story of Jesus different is that it moves beyond the realm of myth alone to enter the realm of history. In other words, it is different because it is *true*. As C.S. Lewis puts it, "The heart of Christianity is a myth which is also a fact. The old myth of the Dying God, *without ceasing to be a myth*, comes down from the heaven of legend and imagination to the earth of history. It *happens*—at a particular date, in a particular place, followed by definable historical consequences."[15] The other stories point to the historical reality of Christ. They are shadows or foreshadows of it.

Lewis traces a progression of the idea of the Christ figure from before the time of the Old Testament to the time of Christ's ministry on earth. First, he says, "you get, scattered through the heathen religions all over the world—but still quite vague and mystical—the idea of a god who is killed and broken and then comes to life again. No one knows where he is supposed to have lived and died; he's not historical." Then in the Old Testament the story begins to come more into focus, until finally, in the New Testament, "the thing really happens. The dying god really appears—as a historical Person, living in a definite place and time."[16]

In Lewis's own conversion to Christianity, his realization that the Christian story was a fulfillment of so many of the hints scattered throughout the pagan myths and stories played a significant role in his ultimate belief in Christ. Lewis, as an atheist, did not *want* to believe, but his "Adversary," God, kept pursuing him. As Lewis's search for the truth continued, he sought answers to questions such as, "Where has religion reached its true maturity?" and "Where, if anywhere, have the hints of all paganism been fulfilled?" Other religions fell short in various ways, but the more he studied Christianity, and the more he sensed God pursuing him, the closer he came to believing that only in Christ had the mythic become real. He wrote, "If ever a myth had become fact, had been incarnated, it would be just like this. And nothing else in all literature was just like this. Myths were like it in one way. Histories were like it in another. But nothing was simply like it."[17]

The myths, the apocalyptic movies, the Christ figures in novels, and stories of other kinds may all point to the truth of Jesus Christ, but that does not mean most people will catch those hints.

The clues of redemption scattered throughout literature, film, and other storytelling modes are easy to ignore. After all, the Bible itself, the bestselling book of all time, tells the story of Jesus and redemption most directly and authoritatively, and people ignore it all the time.

When you read a novel or go to a movie, you may think you're merely relaxing or entertaining yourself or escaping the heavy demands of the day. Many times that may be all that is happening. But sometimes, perhaps more often than you think, maybe part of you is craving more, an encounter not with a fictional tale of redemption but with the Redeemer himself, Jesus. These stories may not be presenting the gospel itself, but are they causing you to lean in its direction? Has God designed the world in such a way that these hints of himself, even in entertainment vehicles that on the surface appear to have nothing to do with him, may help lead you to him? As C.S. Lewis wrote of his own experience, "A young man who wishes to remain a sound Atheist cannot be too careful of his reading. There are traps everywhere—'Bibles laid open, millions of surprises,' as Herbert says, 'fine nets and stratagems.' God is, if I may say it, very unscrupulous."[18]

Go to beaconhillbooks.com/go/nothingiswasted for a free downloadable study guide that includes questions for deeper personal reflection as well as activities for use in a small group setting.

7 ✎ HOW STORYTELLERS CREATE BEAUTY FROM PAIN

Why were the personal lives of many great authors so messed up? That is one of the most common questions I get from students in my literature courses.

Alcoholism, suicide, shattered marriages, financial troubles, and every other kind of imaginable tragedy often pervade the lives of the storytellers I teach. Why should we pay any attention to these writers if they can't even solve their own problems? How could great literature possibly spring from these dysfunctional people?

Some look at these authors' lives and see only brokenness and personal failure, but I see these writers very differently. I look into their lives and see a kind of redemption that gives me hope for my own life.

One common trait I have noticed in the lives of many great writers is that, as children, they often encounter a tragedy, failure, or physical limitation that pushes them toward writing. Without that source of pain, they might never feel the need to write. Feeling cut off from "normal" life in some significant way, they turn to writing as a way of either connecting to the world or making sense of it. The literary works that spring from that pain bring something good out of it.

Humorist James Thurber, for example, who wrote "The Secret Life of Walter Mitty" and other works, had a terrible bow-and-arrow accident as a child that caused blindness in one eye and took him out of the mainstream of boyhood activities. William Faulkner, who would ultimately win the Nobel Prize for literature, had to wear a posture-straightening brace as a boy, which made it hard for him to participate in sports and helped push him toward other pursuits, including storytelling. Alice Walker was shot in the eye as a girl and felt cut off from the regular life of other girls as a result of this disfiguring injury until it was corrected once she was in college. Acclaimed American novelist John Updike suffered an embarrassing skin condition as a child that made him feel set apart from other kids and pushed him toward the more solitary intellectual pursuit of writing. C.S. Lewis had a defective thumb that made sports difficult but opened up writing as a possibility instead.

One important point to make about these childhood difficulties is that those who suffer from them do not become writers *in spite of* their tragedies and illnesses. They turn to writing *because* of them. Writing becomes a way of making sense of their pain, a way of seeking order in the midst of chaos. Without writing, many of these storytellers would have nothing *but* the pain.

In one way or another, much of the great literature of the world springs from pain. Not all of it is from childhood illness and calamity, of course. Some of the suffering happens in adulthood, and some of it must be blamed on the bad actions of the writers themselves. But even then, writing can be a way of transforming those bad actions into at least *something* that is good. The words that spring from the suffering can be life-changing not only for the writer but also for the reader.

When an author turns pain into literature, a redemptive pattern is set in motion. Not only is the writing redemptive for the author, but the literary works that result from this process also allow untold numbers of readers to experience the beauty, inspiration, and wisdom that may grow from life's difficulties. Just as a gifted sculptor might be able to enter a junkyard and use the discarded material there to create a work of art, so a talented writer is able to take the distressing elements of life and weave them into a beautiful work of literature.

The entire creative process, regardless of whether the creativity is expressed through writing, painting, sculpting, acting, or other forms, is suffused with redemption, the transformation of pain into something worthwhile. In his book *Creativity: Flow and The Psychology of Discovery and Invention*, Mihaly Csikszentmihalyi analyzes the creative process based on interviews with ninety-one of the top creative people in fields such as science, art, literature, business, and others. Among the people he interviewed were fourteen Nobel Prize winners in various fields. Novelist Richard Stern said that the "great thing about this kind of work is that every feeling you have, every negative feeling, is in a way precious. It is your building material, it's your stone, it's something you use to build your work. I would say the conversion of the negative is very important." Stern added that even the bad things about himself that he never talks about directly can still help him as a writer: "I can draw strength from that, without talking about them. I can transform them."[1]

For some people, suffering actually unlocks their creativity. Poet Gyorgy Faludy told of a poet friend who wrote atrocious poetry, but then, "suffering in the concentration camps...changed him totally and he wrote wonderful verse. Suffering is not bad: It helps you very much. Do you know a novel about happiness? Or a film about happy people? We are a perverse race, only suffering interests us."[2]

When people speak of the redemption that happens in the literary process, they often are not referring specifically to spiritual salvation in the Christian sense, but at times, with certain works and authors, this literary process does embody ultimate redemption in Jesus Christ. In this chapter I want to look at three great writers—John Updike, Eugene O'Neill, and C.S. Lewis—to show the sometimes surprising ways that pain in the lives of great storytellers is not wasted but is instead transformed into something life-changing for themselves and their readers.

Ugly Skin, Beautiful Stories

Consider John Updike (1932–2009), an American novelist, short story writer, and poet, a two-time Pulitzer Prize winner who became one of the most celebrated writers of his generation. At age six, after an attack of measles in kindergarten, Updike contracted psoriasis, a skin condition that plagued him for decades. Psoriasis, for the unfamiliar, is an uncomfortable and embarrassing condition that causes red and scaly patches to form because of the overproduction of skin. In his 1989 memoir called *Self-Consciousness*, Updike writes of how embarrassed he was about this condition as a boy. Psoriasis gave him the "sense of another presence co-occupying your body and singling you out from the happy herds of healthy, normal mankind."[3] Because of the condition, he didn't learn to swim and avoided the ponds and pools where the other kids hung out during the summer so that he wouldn't have to expose more of his body in public than strictly necessary. He became self-conscious about the condition and did what he could to conceal it from others.

When writing his memoir, Updike still found it painful to write about psoriasis, even though he was in his late fifties and new treatments had cleared him of the condition years earlier. But he realized his suffering had not been wasted. The embarrassment of the years of psoriasis had been redeemed by how the condition had pushed him toward becoming a writer. He says, "Because of my skin, I counted myself out of any of those jobs—salesman, teacher, financier, movie star—that demand being presentable. What did that leave? Becoming a craftsman of some sort, closeted and unseen—perhaps a cartoonist or a writer..."[4]

Because psoriasis played such a role in pushing him toward writing, Updike goes so far as to say that he has mixed feelings about the treatment that freed him from it. He says, "Only psoriasis could have taken a very average little boy, and furthermore a boy who loved the average, the daily, the safely hidden, and made him into a prolific, adaptable, ruthless-enough writer." He calls his creative urge toward relentless literary production a parody of his psoriatic skin's overproduction. Just as psoriasis made his skin thick, he also developed a "thick literary skin, which shrugged off rejection slips and patronizing reviews by the sheaf." Just as he had worried about the spots of psoriasis on his skin, he also agonized over "spots" on his manuscripts, such as typos or factual errors. Psoriasis made him practice a kind of duplicity; he covered his flawed skin under layers of clothes, so that made it easy for him to generate plots in his fiction that exploited duplicity. Updike concludes his reflection on the redeeming qualities of psoriasis with this: "And with my changeable epiderm came a certain transcendent optimism; like a snake, I shed many skins: I had emerged relatively spotless from many a summer and holiday, and the possibility of a 'new life,' in this world or the next, has been ever present to my mind."[5]

Who would have thought that anything positive could come from an ugly skin disease? Certainly it was not inevitable that psoriasis would push Updike toward being a writer. His story could have turned out much differently. The same disease he credits for causing him to set aside other possible career choices in favor of writing could just as easily have caused him to close in on himself and become bitter and resentful. He could have lashed out at God and others because of the unfair circumstances life had dealt him. He could have used his condition as an excuse not to do much of *anything*. The disease, as he describes his situation, ended up pushing him in a productive direction but only because he *chose* to walk through that door of redemption. The disease was not wasted but only because Updike ultimately chose to accept the good that came from it rather than focus only on the pain it brought him.

He didn't consciously adopt this redemptive perspective toward his disease at first, of course. As a kid, he mainly felt the sting of being shut out of activities in which he would have liked to participate, and he felt the humiliation of people staring at him (whether they were actually doing so). But as it became clear that this condition would be something he would have to live with for a long time, perhaps his whole life, he changed his perspective to let it help make him what he otherwise might not have become. Without this disease, he eventually realized, he might never have become a writer, a profession in which he rose to the top of his field. Perhaps he would have chosen one of the other fields that the skin condition (in his mind) closed off to him—salesman or teacher or financier—and would have done only mediocre work.

This is not to say that the psoriasis itself was a good thing. It wasn't. It's a disease that caused suffering. But if, as I have been arguing, reality *bends* toward redemption, then Updike had the wisdom to let that redemption unfold and not block it, as it is so often tempting to do.

Updike's perspective on his struggle with psoriasis seemed to have affected his approach toward other adversities. In *Self-Consciousness*, he writes that he also suffered from other maladies—a tendency to choke on food, a phobia of spiders and insects, and stuttering. About the stuttering, he writes, "As with my psoriasis, the affliction is perhaps not entirely unfortunate." It made him think twice about doing too many public appearances at conferences and elsewhere. As a popular author, he received many such invitations, but he was wary of engaging in too much of this "socially approved yet spiritually corrupting public talking." He concludes, "Being obliging by nature and anxious for social approval, I would never say no if I weren't afraid of stuttering."[6]

Long Day's Journey into Despair?

How low can someone fall and still find redemption?

What about a young man who can't hold a job, flunks out of college, lapses into alcoholism, seethes with bitterness and resentment toward his parents, walks away from his wife and child, contracts malaria and nearly dies during a fruitless quest for gold in a foreign country, nearly starves to death during a trip to South America, gets so despondent that he attempts suicide, and finally contracts tuberculosis at the age of twenty-five in an era when the disease is often fatal?

How much chance would you give such a young man—who, up to that point, had not written much of anything—of becoming one of the greatest dramatists in American literature?

I have just summarized the first twenty-five years in the life of Eugene O'Neill (1888–1953), who, despite his rocky start, would eventually become the most award-winning American playwright in history, winning an unprecedented four Pulitzer Prizes and eventually the Nobel Prize for literature, the highest literary prize in the world.[7] If you had seen him in his early twenties, you probably would have doubted that he would ever accomplish *anything*.

O'Neill's early failures, however, even though they brought pain to himself and others, were not wasted. They were redeemed in ways from which readers and theatergoers today still benefit.

Those failures formed the core of O'Neill's literary material in such plays as *Long Day's Journey into Night* and *The Iceman Cometh*. His years of failure served as material in ways that his later years of success never could.

O'Neill's problems started early—in fact, before he even left the womb. At birth, he weighed eleven pounds! The delivery nearly killed his mother. During her difficult pregnancy, the doctor, not knowing any better, prescribed morphine for her, and she became addicted to it for much of the rest of her life. It was an addiction for which Eugene would feel blamed.

His father was a famous actor, and the family spent much of their lives traveling the country on trains and staying in hotels, a lifestyle Eugene hated. When he was sent to a Catholic boarding school, he wasn't used to being around other children, so he rebelled. His mother's addiction was kept hidden from him until he was fifteen years old, when, on one fog-shrouded night, having run out of morphine, she ran screaming from the house in her nightdress and tried to drown herself in the river. Learning of her addiction and the family's concealment of it from him fueled his cynicism and isolation.

When he grew up, his family got him into Princeton. Sounds good, right? He read all day long. Unfortunately, none of his reading was related to the courses he was taking. His schedule consisted of reading all day and drinking all night, and after one year, they kicked him out. He didn't care. After that, he drifted around New York, where his father's standing in the theater got him in free at all the Broadway shows, and where there were plenty of bars to get drunk in.

At the age of twenty, he fell in love. However, this was not a happy development in his story. His father was particularly alarmed about the affair. His son had no means to support a wife. Eugene's father was well off and feared the girl might be after his money. The solution Eugene's parents came up with was to get their son as far away from the girl as possible, and the opportunity that presented itself was a friend's expedition to Honduras to search for gold. Eugene willingly agreed to the unlikely venture, but before he left, he foiled his parents' plans by secretly marrying the girl, who became pregnant.

In Honduras he found no gold, and after a year of slicing his way through the jungle, all he brought home with him was a case of malaria. Back in New York, he was not prepared for the demands of marriage and his new baby boy (who, by the way, weighed only ten and a half pounds at birth). He didn't move in with his wife and child. Instead, he moved to his parents' apartment, but the jungle experience had unhinged him, and one night, alone and disturbed, he pulled out his machete from Honduras and hacked up his parents' home. They came home to find their son passed out drunk on the floor, his machete beside him, their furniture in shreds.

Since New York wasn't working out, Eugene signed on to work on the crew of a ship bound for Argentina. Once he got there, he quickly ran out of money. He slept on park benches and adopted a diet that consisted of only one item: beer. That lifestyle was starving him, so he signed on to the crew of another ship and headed back to New York. He didn't do much there except go to the theater on his father's free pass and hang out at his favorite saloon. He liked this bar so much that he moved into it. It had a flophouse on the second floor that consisted of a row of windowless cells just large enough for a cot and a chair. The mattresses were made of straw so they could be easily thrown out after the men soiled them. The rent was three dollars a month. The unemployed Eugene lived on the dollar-per-day allowance his father provided.

His next couple years went by in this saloon, with occasional jobs on ships. His wife divorced him. Still living in his flophouse in his mid-twenties, with few prospects for a satisfying future,

O'Neill fell into despair and attempted suicide by taking an overdose of drugs in his cell. A friend rescued him, the drugs wore off, and he continued to drift through life.

Notice that, although O'Neill was to become one of the most influential playwrights in American history, so far in his story no mention has been made of writing. Was he secretly keeping a notebook by his bed at the flophouse or in his bunk on the ships? Were the early drafts of the plays that would someday make him famous slowly taking shape? No. Because of his resentment toward his father, he had no desire to work in the theater, and he hadn't written any plays.

His directionless existence had hit a low point, but it was to get even worse. When he was twenty-five years old, O'Neill was diagnosed with tuberculosis. In 1913, that disease was often fatal. He went to a clinic specializing in treating tuberculosis and doubted he would ever come out alive.

The scare of tuberculosis jolted O'Neill into contemplating the direction of his life in a way that nothing else had. Like Updike's psoriasis, O'Neill's more serious condition forced him out of life's routine and made him reflect on important realities in ways he might never have done without the crisis. Redemption crept in. He decided to live. He decided to become a playwright.

Having made this decision, he acted on it immediately. He changed not only his behavior but also his identity. Up to this time he had played the role of drifter and drunk. Now he identified himself—and acted—as a writer. The decision redeemed his past not simply because he decided to step away from his past and become something else but also because what had once been merely a long, embarrassing, and harmful string of failures and pointless episodes now became writing material. In a strange way, all the chaos of his life had been research. He used it and, to some extent, transformed it through the power of writing.

Keep in mind that the redemption I am referring to was not a full-fledged, spiritual salvation. It did not touch on every aspect of his life. It points *toward* that more complete transformation but is not in itself that salvation. O'Neill did not ask forgiveness from his wife, son, parents, or others he had hurt, did not turn to Christ for salvation, did not repent of all the ways of thinking and behaving that led him into such difficulty. Those avenues of complete redemption were available to him, but he did not seek them. Still, his story, like so many others, shows that redemption is such a powerful force in the universe that it can enter the life of someone even when that person has sunk to the bottom. It entered O'Neill's life only in the very limited way that he allowed, but even that was powerful.

Once O'Neill decided to become a playwright, he wasted no time. He immersed himself in the works of other playwrights. He sketched out ideas. He wrote dialogue, then scenes. Day after day, week after week, he worked. He wrote more than a dozen plays in the first two years after he started.

His health improved. After five months, he was released from the clinic. He kept writing. He took all that confusion and failure and adventure from his early life and transformed it into art. Remember the gold-hunting trip to Honduras? He uses that in his play *The Emperor Jones.* The work on the ships? That shows up in plays like *Anna Christie* and *The Hairy Ape.* The seedy bar and flophouse where he lived? Immortalized in *The Iceman Cometh.* The actor father and morphine-addicted mother? Those show up in *Long Day's Journey into Night.*

After he started writing plays, the rest of O'Neill's life was certainly not a happily-ever-after story. Although he achieved tremendous literary success, he continued to struggle with marital problems with three wives, difficult relationships with his children, a neurological disorder that made writing and functioning in other ways very difficult, and many other challenges. Spiritually, O'Neill rejected Christianity early on, largely because of the morphine addiction of his devoutly Catholic mother. The fact that her faith helped her confront that addiction later in life came too late to change O'Neill's mind about Christianity. He stepped into one kind of redemption but away from another.

Literary success did not solve all of O'Neill's problems or meet all of his deep spiritual needs. However, his story is a powerful example of how early failures in life can be transformed, and how that principle seems to be built into the very way life is structured. I teach O'Neill to students who are the age O'Neill was when he was at his lowest point, with seemingly no hope or future. Many of these students, though usually not as troubled or down and out as O'Neill, have nevertheless silently concluded that their lives may not amount to much, that the barriers and limitations they sense all around them are essentially what will define them. Many are willing to settle for just getting by. I want to tell them, "Look, redemption is all around us, even for someone as lost as O'Neill was at your age. Step into it! Your weaknesses and failures are not the end of your story. They can be transformed."

Lives Fueled by Hope, Not Inevitability

Students who read the works of many of the great writers often get the idea that the success of these writers was all but inevitable. I used to think that way myself. *Of course* people like O'Neill and John Updike would become writers and find success. Wouldn't their gift be obvious to themselves and everyone else? But studying their lives shows they had the same kinds of self-doubt, self-consciousness, failures, rejections, false starts, and endless obstacles that plague all of us. Most of them also had naysayers in their lives who scoffed at their aspirations and flatly predicted their failure.

It was in no way *inevitable* that any of them would overcome those problems. It would have been easy for Updike to let his self-consciousness extend to his writing and not let anyone see it, just as he didn't want them to see his psoriatic skin. It would have been easy for O'Neill to concentrate only on getting cured from tuberculosis as he lay in that clinic.

The writers themselves often agreed with those who didn't believe in their ability—up to a point. But their *drive* to write was so strong that insecurity or fear of failure could not overcome it. They agonized and second-guessed themselves, but they kept writing. Sometimes success took years. None of this is to say that their success or anyone else's is guaranteed simply by persistence. Sometimes failure is redeemed in ways we don't expect. A person may fail as a writer but find that effort redeemed in some other field or endeavor.

But for those who did achieve their desire to become authors, they were often as surprised by their success as everyone else and could never have predicted or planned the winding paths that got them there. Often the very circumstances that should have stopped them ended up being the events that made their writing careers possible. Sometimes the personal traits their scoffers held against them ended up being the very characteristics that make them the most distinctive as writers.

Moving from Literary Redemption to Ultimate Redemption

Although some people block any redemption of their harsh circumstances and others settle for a limited kind, some authors have followed the hints of redemption all the way to Jesus, who eventually permeates not only their lives but also their literary works.

C.S. Lewis is such a writer.

In 2013 I was assigned to write a review of Devin Brown's spiritual biography of C.S. Lewis, *A Life Observed*, and as I read through the details of his life, I was struck repeatedly by how many hardships, failures, and bad circumstances were thrown at him that might easily have pushed him in an entirely different direction. I have long admired Lewis's books, and *Mere Christianity* in particular influenced me to solidify my faith when I was a doubting college student. I loved the *Narnia* books and *The Screwtape Letters* and other works. From what little I knew about Lewis when I first encountered his books, he seemed to have lived a life I could only envy: He taught at Oxford, wrote books people loved, helped numerous people grapple with deep questions of their faith. From a distance, the course of his life looked smooth and inevitable, but it was nothing of the kind.

Lewis's life was filled with difficulties, large and small, that were not wasted but, rather, were redeemed by helping push him toward Jesus, toward writing, and toward the position of Christian influence that he eventually filled. His brother, Warnie, tells of one seemingly trivial difficulty that he believes played an important role in Lewis's development as a writer—bad weather. Lewis grew up in Ireland, where rain was frequent and where his parents were afraid of the boys being exposed too much to the dampness. That meant the boys had to spend an extraordinary amount of time indoors, watching the rain hit the windowpanes of their home.

The bad weather was not wasted, however. It turned the boys' attention from outdoor activities to activities of the imagination. Warnie says that as the rain fell, "we always had pencils, paper, chalk and paintboxes, and this recurring imprisonment gave us occasion and stimulus to develop the habit of creative imagination."[8]

As Lewis grew up, he was hindered from performing well in sports because of another problem, a defective thumb. His thumb's upper joint was not formed properly and would not bend as it should, limiting his athletic skill. The thumb also limited his ability to work with tools and perform a variety of other tasks. Lewis himself says about his abnormality, "It was this that forced me to write." As a boy, he was not happy about this misfortune but later wrote that he had no idea of "the world of happiness" into which the defect would actually admit him.[9]

Lewis knew from an early age that the academic life was the only one he was really suited for, but he was almost blocked from it. Although he was a brilliant student in many ways and received a prestigious scholarship that would cover many of his expenses, one of the entrance exams included a section on math, Lewis's worst subject. The first time he took it, he failed. He still received a provisional admission then was given time to study for the exam again. A few months later, he retook the exam and flunked it a second time. As biographer Devin Brown explains, "With this second failure, it became clear that Lewis's deficiencies in math were far more serious than anyone had admitted, and the world came very close to losing C.S. Lewis as a scholar, teacher, and writer."[10]

Ironically, Lewis's failure in math was redeemed by another calamity, World War I. After spending only about eight weeks as a college student, Lewis joined the British Army and served in France, where he was wounded. After the war, Lewis was able to attend Oxford without having to worry about his math problems because that exam was waived for war veterans. If it had not been waived, Lewis likely would have failed the exam again and not gotten into Oxford. That might have cost him his chance at an academic career, which most likely would have meant he would never have written the books that have influenced so many millions of readers.

After Lewis finished his undergraduate studies and received his BA degree, he hoped to start an academic career but was unable to find a job in philosphy, the field in which he was trained. As one job possibility after another passed him by, he began to believe he might not be able to secure a position in academia. Faced with this disappointment, Lewis decided to spend one more year getting a degree in English. That decision changed the rest of his life. It led to his teaching career in literature, his writing of scholarly works in that field, and his reading of Christian literary classics that helped influence him to become a Christian later on.

The philosophy training, however, was certainly not wasted. The combination of philosophy and English proved valuable for the kinds of popular works Lewis eventually wrote. As Brown points out, if Lewis had gone into philosophy right away and not studied English, he might never have written works of fiction such as *The Screwtape Letters* or the *Narnia* books. On the other hand, if he had not studied philosophy, he might not have been equipped to write books such as *Miracles*, *The Problem of Pain*, or *Mere Christianity*.

Even Lewis's Atheism Was Not Wasted

Considering where C.S. Lewis ended up—as one of the most influential Christian authors of his era—his early atheism might sound like a huge barrier toward reaching that outcome. However, as Lewis scholar David Downing explains, even Lewis's atheism was ultimately useful. He says, "A careful look at Lewis's early years reveals that he did not become an effective defender of the faith *despite* the fact that he spent so many years as an unbeliever. Rather, his Christian books are compelling precisely *because* he spent so many years as an unbeliever. He understood atheism."[11]

The point is not simply that Lewis *overcame* all his adversities and failures. The point is that the difficulties actually ended up serving to make him the great writer and Christian thinker he became. The adversities were used for good. With so much redemption in his own life, Lewis chose to write works that themselves served redemptive purposes, leading people to Christ. Some works, such as *Mere Christianity*, confront issues of faith directly. Other books, such as the *Narnia* books and other works of fiction, take a more indirect approach toward Christian themes. In the *Narnia* novels, for instance, Aslan is a Christ figure, and Christian themes are prevalent in the story, but readers may enjoy the *Narnia* books even if they never draw those parallels or have any knowledge of Christianity. The books may, however, provoke a longing for Christ. As Lewis scholar Peter Schakel puts it, the *Narnia* books "are, mainly, children's books, and Lewis seems to have intended that they awaken in a child a love for Aslan and for goodness which can grow, as the child matures, into love for and acceptance of Christ."[12]

Millions of readers have drawn closer to Christ—and some have confronted him for the first time—because of C.S. Lewis's writing. As Lewis faced each of his adversities—bad weather, deformed thumbs, a world war, academic failures, blocked opportunities, even his own atheism—he could never have imagined how God would weave them into a tapestry of redemption that would be soul-saving for others. None of it was wasted.

Go to beaconhillbooks.com/go/nothingiswasted for a free downloadable study guide that includes questions for deeper personal reflection as well as activities for use in a small group setting.

8 ⮞ SOME UNEXPECTED BENEFITS OF DEATH

*Very truly I tell you, unless a kernel of wheat falls to
the ground and dies, it remains only a single seed. But
if it dies, it produces many seeds. John 12:24*

As a kid, I used to love the story "Jack and the Beanstalk." I identified strongly with Jack, who disobeys his mother and gets in
trouble for it. I had been there many times. Jack and his mother
are so poor that she sends him off to sell their only cow. The sale
has huge significance for them—they need the money to survive.
Jack shoulders a big responsibility as he leads that cow away to sell
it, but the transaction should be fairly simple: Sell the cow; bring
the money home.

On the way to the market, however, Jack comes across an old
man who offers him something more promising than mere money for the precious animal. The man offers him magic beans. If
planted, they will grow high into the sky, and who knows where
such a beanstalk might lead? If Jack were a sensible and obedient
son, he would simply say no to this offer. His mother has given

him a clear mandate, and he should sell that cow and get the money. The old man is probably a scam artist. He's offering beans! But Jack takes the beans, and when I experienced this story as a child, I always cheered him on, despite the risk. Who wants mere money when you can have magic beans?

Then comes the horrible part of the story, as I saw it. Jack has to go home and explain his disobedience to Mother. I would have hated that trip back home, trying to come up with an explanation that would mollify her, imagining her anger and the possible punishments.

Jack's encounter with Mother, as expected, does not go well. Their financial situation is desperate, and Jack has traded their only valuable possession for a bunch of worthless beans. In anger she flings the beans into the dirt and sends Jack to bed without any supper.

Jack's mother expects that to be the end of the story. After all, when you throw something away, you expect that to finish it.

In this case, however, Jack's mother has thrown away beans—or seeds, essentially—and seeds are different from other things you throw away. Seeds are counterintuitive. Most of us are so familiar with them that we forget how unusual they really are. Usually when you toss something in the dirt, or bury it in the ground, that means you are either killing it or hiding it or disposing of it. With seeds, it's different. Seeds absolutely depend on that burial, that particular kind of destruction, in order to produce anything. Unless you do what looks like killing them, you'll never get anywhere. You'll be stuck with hard little blobs that don't seem worth much at all.

Jack's mother doesn't get that. She doesn't share Jack's faith in transformation. She looks at the beans in his hand and sees only beans. Jack sees what they might become through the magic of transformational destruction and resurrection.

By throwing the seeds into the dirt, the very place they need to be, Jack's mother has inadvertently set in motion a process that will make her rich. When she and her son wake up the next morning, a giant beanstalk has grown high into the sky. Jack climbs it, faces down the threats of the mean giant who lives in the kingdom at the top, and gets hold of enough riches to keep himself and his mother financially secure for the rest of their lives.

Does the Seed Really Have to Die?

Imagine if the story had gone differently. In this alternate version, after his mother flings the beans into the dirt, Jack secretly runs out and retrieves them. He holds the precious beans in his hands for hours. He goes to sleep with them under his pillow. The next morning, he hides them in a box in the closet, where his mother won't find them. Each day he takes them out and admires them, running them through his fingers and holding them up to the light, and then he puts them back in the box. The end.

Not much of a story, is it? This version would pretty much confirm Jack's mother's attitude about the stupidity of trading the cow for these beans. What good are magic beans if all they're going to do is sit in a box and look pretty? Besides which, beans aren't even that pretty. He could always cook the beans and eat them, but there aren't very many, so that paltry meal would be over pretty quickly and wouldn't be very satisfying. No, the only way for Jack's beans to pay off is if they are planted and grow that big beanstalk.

When Jesus says in John 12:24 that the only way to turn a single kernel of wheat into *lots* of seeds is to let it fall to the ground and *die*, he is illustrating a spiritual principle that he teaches in several ways throughout the gospels. Right after giving the illustration of the seed falling to ground and dying, he says, "Anyone who loves their life will lose it, while anyone who hates their life in this world will keep it for eternal life" (John 12:25).

Nature itself, Jesus shows us, embodies this spiritual truth that some things have to die to what they *are* in order to become what they were *intended* to be. The seed, when it is buried in the dirt, doesn't simply grow bigger as a seed. You don't have gigantic seeds pop up in your garden; you have plants spring up that started as seeds. In order for that process to occur, the seed must die to its original form. It will break apart as a seed.

That part of the process is normally hidden from view, down in the ground, but if you witnessed it without understanding the way all this worked, you might think it looked pretty bad for the seed, all torn up like that. At first, the seed would look much worse than when you first buried it. The whole thing would look like a terrible failure. Only time and nature's processes will confirm that this complete shattering of the seed is not a failure but a triumph. It will grow a plant that may produce life-giving fruit, not to mention more seeds that may produce even more plants. The seeming destruction of the seed is not wasted. It is ultimately not even a destruction. It is a redemptive transformation.

What Jesus Knew about the Necessity of His Own Death

When Jesus tells his disciples about the kernel of wheat falling to the ground and dying so it can rise up and produce many seeds, he is revealing a general spiritual truth, but he is also referring to something more specific. He is telling them about himself. He is preparing them for his own death and resurrection. They need this explanation from Jesus because what is about to happen to him is not what they have in mind for him. It is not how they think he should go about things. Repeatedly throughout the gospels, the disciples either seem not to understand that Jesus is going to be killed, or when they do understand, they try to deny it. At one point Jesus teaches them quite bluntly that "the Son of Man must suffer many things and be rejected by the elders, chief priests and the teachers of the law, and that he must be killed and after three days rise again" (Mark 8:31).

Peter is horrified by this thought and actually takes Jesus aside and rebukes him. Jesus reacts harshly. "Get behind me, Satan!" he tells Peter. "You do not have in mind the concerns of God, but merely human concerns" (Mark 8:33). Peter, understandably but wrongly, doesn't want the seed to die. He wants Jesus to live.

Jesus knows that, without his own death, he cannot fulfill his purpose. The heart of the gospel is that the blood of Jesus Christ pays for our sins and makes us right with God. Jesus knows there is no way around that death. Jesus "was delivered over to death for our sins and was raised to life for our justification," Romans 4:25 says. Without Jesus's death, there is no salvation. But the seed doesn't stay dead. Without the resurrection, there is no salvation either. The seed is buried. It dies. But it rises in glory and splendor. It produces fruit. It produces new seeds. Christians follow a *living* Jesus Christ, who will live with us for eternity. We believe we will be resurrected when we die, just as Jesus was.

Jesus shows that this transformative cycle operates at many levels, in nature with the seeds, in his own life with his death and resurrection, and in the lives of his followers as they follow his principle that in order to save their lives they have to lose them. Giving one's life to Christ when one becomes a Christian is such a death and resurrection. Scripture teaches that "if anyone is in Christ, the new creation has come: The old has gone, the new is here!" (2 Corinthians 5:17). To become a Christian, you step away from your old life. You repent of your sin, and you let your old identity die, so you can grow into a new one. You become a new branch connected to the Vine named Jesus Christ.

But these transformative deaths and resurrections do not stop at conversion. Rather, the Christian life is a series of transformative deaths and resurrections. Prejudices, limitations, false self-concepts, self-centered motivations, illusions of self-sufficiency, and many other seeds have to be buried in the ground and allowed to die so that Christlike motivations can sprout and produce good fruit.

As life-giving as this process sounds, it is always accompanied by a dangerous negative force that has the potential to undermine it—resistance.

I Like My Seed the Way It Is

I want to make a prediction: No matter how positive all this talk of seeds and plants may sound at the moment, when you are called on to bury your seed to let it die so it can be transformed into what it was meant to be, you won't want to do it. Seed burial, rather than seed preservation, is so counterintuitive, and often so painful, that resistance is built into it. It helps to anticipate that resistance so that, with God's help, we can overcome it when it happens.

It is probably safe to say that no one who has ever lived has been clearer about his or her purpose on this earth than Jesus Christ. He knew what he had to do. Still, even Jesus wrestles with resistance as he faces his moment of truth. Only three verses after Jesus tells his disciples about the necessity of the kernel of wheat falling to the ground and dying, he says, "Now my heart is troubled, and what shall I say? 'Father, save me from this hour'? No, it was for this very reason I came to this hour. Father, glorify your name!" (John 12:27-28). Jesus knows the seed has to die, but that does not lessen the agony.

On the night before his crucifixion, Jesus prays, "Father, if you are willing, take this cup from me; yet not my will, but yours be done." Jesus is in such agony at the thought of what is to come that his sweat is "like drops of blood falling to the ground," and an angel from heaven comes to strengthen him (Luke 22:42-44).

Resistance. Agony. If even Jesus, with his clarity of purpose, fought so much resistance within himself at the thought of the burial and death of the seed, then what chance do any of us have at escaping that same resistance when our own seeds must die? Certainly Peter can't stand up to this force when he rebukes Jesus. Likewise, many people, when faced with the prospect of turning to Christ in repentance, hold back as resistance flares up in them. Deep down, they may long to turn to Jesus, but another part of them seeks to preserve the seed as it is. For Christians who feel called to risk burying the seeds of who they are in order to let Christ grow them into something new and more fruitful, resistance may rise up to declare, "The seed is fine as it is. Look, it is strong, solid, filled with potential. Do not let it go."

Sometimes the fear and resistance are simply so strong that, without God's help, we can't let go of that seed to let it die. We cling to it desperately even though a part of us knows we need to let it go. Without God's intervention, we are doomed to failure.

The good news is that God sometimes does intervene. Like Jack's mother, he enters the story to fling the seed into the dirt, where it can do some good. The bad news is that, like Jack, we will probably not be grateful for that intervention at first. It will feel like punishment. It will hurt. Like Jack when his mother first throws out his seeds, we may at first feel angry and confused. But when we see the results, we may change our minds.

A Resistant Seed Named Jonah

One of the great biblical stories of resistance is found in the story of Jonah. One way to think of that story is that Jonah is a resistant seed who has to be forcefully buried deep in the insides of the great fish, prepared for that purpose. After his "death" inside that fish, an utterly transformed Jonah is vomited onto the ground, where he bears tremendous fruit.

But let's look at Jonah a little more carefully.

Jonah's life would be much easier if he obeys God from the start, but he simply does not want to do what God has asked. He thinks God's command is a bad idea. He resists.

Looking at Jonah's story from the distance of so many centuries, it may be hard to see why Jonah resists God so fiercely. God's command is simple: Jonah must go to Nineveh and preach against it because of its wickedness.

Jonah not only refuses to do so; he also takes his protest against this command even further. He takes off in the opposite direction, boarding a ship that is sailing for Tarshish in order to flee the Lord. He doesn't flee because he likes Nineveh and is reluctant to condemn it. On the contrary, he senses that if he does obey God and warn the city of its impending destruction, the people might actually listen to him and repent. Jonah knows that mercy and forgiveness are integral aspects of God's character and that, if the Ninevites repent, this merciful and forgiving God will probably save them. Jonah wants no part of helping the Ninevites. He thinks they *deserve* destruction. He runs away as fast as he can.

Jonah may sound a little hard-hearted about this, but it might help to consider the people he thinks his prophecy might spare. They are truly malicious people who carry out monstrous acts. The most sadistic Hollywood horror movie could not outdo the Ninevites for thinking up horrific ways to torture and kill. They decapitate people, put the heads on poles, and make the friends of the murdered people walk around carrying those poles. They cut off people's hands and feet, they cut off noses and ears, they gouge out eyes. They burn people alive. They display ghastly piles of heads for all to see.[1] They dream up a whole list of other tortures as well. They also enslave people they overthrow, including some Israelites. They are truly despicable people. Jonah wants them dead.

Even if Jonah could set aside his dread that the Ninevites might repent and be spared God's wrath, obeying God's command to prophesy to them still holds big dangers for him. One likely outcome is that these violent people will not take kindly to his condemnation and will simply kill him. Or maybe they will do horrible things to him, *then* kill him. None of the imaginable outcomes sounds good to Jonah. Running away sounds better.

It may be wise not to be too harsh toward Jonah's rebellion in this case. As some commentators have pointed out, he runs away not from a motivation to undermine justice or do evil but rather to do what he thinks will *establish* justice. He is acting in accordance with what he believes to be God's way of handling evil. In acting the way he does, however, he is ignoring that other aspect of God's character that he's fully aware of—mercy. Rather than trusting God's full character, Jonah decides to take matters into his own hands. As commentator James Bruckner puts it, "Jonah is being faithful to what he knows to be God's word (strict justice) when God asks him to contravene that word with a new word. God's new word is a controversial word (even among believers today)."[2] Eventually, of course, Jonah relents and does things God's way, but it will take God's powerful thwarting to convince Jonah that God really does want this word preached to Nineveh.

Serving God on His Own Terms

When Jonah boards his ship, he is in a situation to which many of us can relate in our relationships with God. We *want* to follow God, but we want to do it our own way. Our obedience and trust extend only so far. If God veers too far from what we think the mission should be, we're tempted to try our own methods to bring about the outcomes we prefer. We might flee, as Jonah does, simply shutting out God's voice, straying from our faith. Or we might choose other methods of rebellion, such as rationalizing, procrastinating, sidestepping, or denying. We may think, *Surely God could not be pushing me in this direction. Surely my way of thinking about this situation is better.* At that point, our only hope, like Jonah's, is that God will deal with us mercifully, finding a way to block our path until we come to our senses.

Jonah has no one but himself to blame for the predicament in which he finds himself, but God immediately goes to work to bring about Jonah's ultimate redemption. God hurls a violent storm at the ship. Notice that God is thwarting Jonah here but not destroying him. God still believes in his prophet, and even though he is creating an uncomfortable situation for him, his ultimate goal is to save Jonah, just as he intends to save the Ninevites if they repent.

As often happens, Jonah's disobedience affects not only himself; it also threatens to drag others down with him. When the storm hits, the sailors will do anything to save themselves. They cry out to their gods. They throw cargo overboard to lighten the ship. Nothing works. They find Jonah—asleep!—below deck, and they cast lots to see who among them has caused this calamity. Jonah is the one. He doesn't deny it. He admits that he is running from the Lord. When they ask what can be done to save them, Jonah tells them to throw him overboard.

They don't want to do it. They try to get back to land instead, but that doesn't work. Jonah's plan seems to be their last hope. They fear God's reprisal if they kill Jonah by tossing him into the sea, but they have no choice. They throw Jonah overboard, praying God will not kill them for doing so. To their relief, the sea calms down.

That very well could be the end of the story and the end of Jonah. But God's redemption is already filling this story. For one thing, the sailors, who have served other gods, now turn to Jonah's God, offering a sacrifice and making vows. Their harrowing ordeal has not been wasted; it has led them to an encounter with the God they now revere.

Jonah also gets a fresh start. Think of God's options for dealing with Jonah in this story. Early on, he could simply let Jonah go to Tarshish and forget about him. Jonah would live out his life far from God and die in rebellion. But God cares too much about Jonah to let that happen, so he intervenes with the storm. Another option God has is simply to let Jonah drown once he is thrown overboard, which is what Jonah and the sailors all expect. On the other hand, God could let the ship get back to land without the necessity of Jonah's being tossed into the sea. The sailors try mightily to get their ship to shore, but they can't do it.

Instead, God chooses something in between. Rather than destroy Jonah or simply let him go, God handles Jonah's resistance in a way that will allow him the best chance to come to terms with God's command and change his mind about his rebellion.

More Than Survival Is at Stake

God prepares a great fish to swallow Jonah. It's not just that some big whale happens to come along and swallow him. God has *prepared* this particular fish for this particular purpose. It's his way of rescuing Jonah, but God has more than rescue in mind. There are plenty of simpler ways to rescue him, after all. Jonah is going to have to spend three days and three nights inside this creature—which obviously gets Jonah's attention in a way that nothing else can. He will have to come to terms with God one way or the other. To return to the seed analogy, the seed of Jonah is being planted in the soil of the great fish. The seed will die in that soil, but in what sense? Will it simply perish, as seeds sometimes do, or will it die in the sense of losing its current form then emerging from the soil as a new and productive plant?

The method God uses with Jonah is admittedly unusual. You shouldn't expect that God will prepare a great fish to swallow *you*. But you also shouldn't be surprised if God plants you in the dirt in a way that is inconvenient and even painful. God may put you in a place that is not where you wanted or expected to be. Does Jonah ever imagine he will be stuck in the belly of a fish?

It almost certainly is difficult to feel positive about this process while it is happening. Imagine yourself literally stuck in the belly of a great fish. What would it even feel like? The darkness, the sliminess, the terror? Would it feel as if God had your best interests at heart as you experienced this horror? God is using the fish not to make Jonah suffer but, rather, to rescue him, to keep him from drowning, to eventually bring him out of that fish as a better, more obedient prophet and person.

Just as God has a number of options how to handle Jonah's rebellion, Jonah has a number of options how to respond to being swallowed by the fish. Despair is one option. Panic is another. Anger at God for putting him in such a horrible situation is also an option.

Instead, Jonah chooses gratitude. He is grateful for his rescue, strange though it is. Rather than focusing on the fact that he is encased inside the guts of this fish, he instead thanks God for not letting him drown in the sea. Jonah is already looking ahead. He doesn't expect that God is going to leave him there in that fish. He doesn't expect to die there. God has saved him, and Jonah is thankful. "But I, with shouts of grateful praise, will sacrifice to you," Jonah says in that fish. "What I have vowed I will make good. I will say, 'Salvation comes from the LORD'" (Jonah 2:9).

I'm not sure I could muster such optimism in that dark and slimy place, but Jonah's faith in God's deliverance is now so strong that he gives thanks as if his full rescue has already come.

Getting Vomited Up Toward a Brighter Future

Once this important spiritual work inside Jonah is done, he gets vomited up onto dry land. Not exactly a triumphant way to emerge, but Jonah is now back on track. God gives him a second chance to go to Nineveh and proclaim the message he was supposed to deliver in the first place.

This time, Jonah does it. The outcome is just as Jonah feared. The evil people of Nineveh repent, and God saves them from destruction. Jonah's story has become one of redemption, through and through. He is saved, the sailors on the ship are saved, and the people of Nineveh turn to God and are spared.

Happy ending, right? It looks that way to everyone but Jonah. He is still angry about the Ninevites not getting the punishment they deserve. He pours out his anger to God, pretty much telling him, "I told you so," before adding, "I knew that you are a gracious and compassionate God, slow to anger and abounding in love, a God who relents from sending calamity" (Jonah 4:2).

Exactly. Jonah is right about God's propensity for love. Without it, we would all be lost. Jonah is happy to accept God's forgiveness when it comes to his own rescue, but he is angry when God confers the same compassion on Jonah's enemies. He is so angry he wants to die. Even now, God keeps working with Jonah to change his heart about forgiveness. By the end of the book, it is not clear whether Jonah has yet been convinced, but for us as readers, it is clear that God has changed Jonah in ways that have given the prophet a second chance to obey and follow God. Jonah does the right thing, even though, like many of us who follow the Lord, he doesn't always fully understand or approve of God's methods.

None of us can know the full significance of our own stories while we are living them. Whenever God is busy growing me into something new, I probably will be concentrating only on how that affects *me*. But who else may be watching? Who else may be affected because God's work on me put me in a place where I otherwise would not have been?

Jonah's story has significance far beyond what he can imagine. It is not only about him, or even only about him and the sailors and the Ninevites. Hundreds of years later, Jesus himself draws Jonah's redemptive story into his own. When Jesus's skeptics come to him and ask for a miraculous sign, Jesus answers that no sign will be given to them except the sign of the prophet Jonah. "For as Jonah was three days and three nights in the belly of a huge fish, so the Son of Man will be three days and three nights in the heart of the earth" (Matthew 12:40). Although Jonah's story is significant in itself, it gains even more importance as Jesus connects it to his own death and resurrection.

Just as Jonah was thrown into the deep then entombed for three days in the great fish, which should have killed him, so Jesus will be killed and will descend into death for three days, from which even his closest followers do not expect him to emerge. But what looks like a catastrophe is actually the death—and resurrection—that will bring salvation to all who put their trust in Christ. Jonah, the prophet who spent so much of his time being angry at God, is given the privilege of being part of that story.

The Seed Is Going to Die, But Will It Produce Anything?

Seeds don't last forever.

Imagine yourself holding a seed in your hand. Turn it over. Feel the waxy hardness of it. Consider its potential. Think about what it might become if you were to sink it down into the soil and give it water and light. The benefits of planting the seed should be obvious. What a remarkable fact of creation that so much life can spring from such a small object!

Yet fear may hinder the planting process. I know the seed has to be buried and die before it can produce, but part of me is still tempted to hold back. What if I drop it in the ground and it doesn't grow? What if it dies down there and stays dead? What if I plant it wrong, too shallow or too deep? What if the conditions for its growth are all wrong, in ways that I don't understand? Maybe I should just hold on to this seed. At least that way I still have *something*.

Life is a series of seed-planting decisions. Each time I push a seed into the ground, I risk failure. I also invite the disruption and pain that comes from the seed being ripped apart in order to allow new life to spring forth. At an earlier stage of my own life, for example, I had to decide whether to plant the seed to attend graduate school. About half the students who entered the doctoral program never made it through. Assuming I got accepted somewhere, did I want to risk being one who failed? Did I want to invest all those years, all that effort, into something with such a shaky promise of paying off? Would the sacrifices of living in a small room, on almost nothing, for several years, with no guarantee of a job at the end, be worth it?

I placed that seed in the ground, and the plant grew. The costs were heavy in terms of time, a sometimes crushing workload, and lack of money, but the relationships, the life-changing education, and the career that resulted were branches of the sturdy tree that sprang from the planting of that tiny seed.

Marriage was another seed I held in my hand. Should I risk it? I loved the woman I wanted to marry, but so many marriages fail. Was I really cut out for it? What if I made a mess of it?

Writing was another life seed I gripped tightly in my fist. I felt compelled, even called, to do it, but it is another area that, in general, is fraught with more failure than success. Did I want to plant my seed into the soil of months or years of writing when there was no guarantee anything would come of it? Would it be better to plant a seed that was more of a sure thing?

Faith in Christ was another seed I held in my hand. I deeply sensed the Holy Spirit drawing me, but what if I was wrong? Did I want to risk turning over my life to a God whom so many other people are convinced does not even exist?

With many of these seeds, the risks were certainly real. Not every seed produces a healthy plant. Some seeds stay dead in the ground. I have a large stack of rejections of writing projects and job applications to prove it. But what about the seed that remains in the hand? What happens to it?

In "Jack and the Beanstalk," Jack's mother angrily flings away the beans. My temptation is usually not to fling the seeds away; for me, the temptation is to hold on to them and think, *Someday I'm going to plant this, when the time is right.* I want to hold back, not commit myself, preserve my options.

A spiritual life of *drifting* has a powerful appeal to me. Drifting in general sounds pretty good to me right now, while I am in a phase of life in which I face many demands. The temptation that sometimes hits me is to ease up, stop pushing so hard. I want to do the minimum to get by—get the bills paid, take care of my kids and their needs, make sure my wife is cared for, get my work done, but go easy. I want to hide myself in a place where I don't have to say yes to much, don't get put into uncomfortable situations, and don't put myself out there where I could end up looking like a fool. I don't want to have to think too much, or get drawn into other people's difficulties too much, or give too much, or love too much, or sacrifice too much, or risk too much. I want to bounce the seed up and down in my hand.

I have sometimes envisioned this kind of drifting life and have asked God to give it to me. I don't sense God pushing me in that direction, though. On the contrary, I sense him wanting me fully alive, fully engaged—learning new things, embracing people, confronting challenges. He wants me to risk looking like a fool. He wants me to challenge my old ways of thinking. He wants me to surrender my commitment to comfort. He wants me to really *see* those around me and to love them. I don't sense a letup anytime soon.

One way or another, every seed dies. It can die in my hand, or it can die in the ground, where its current structure will be destroyed and it will transform into something far mightier and more useful. Only that second type of death is redemptive. The first death, of a seed clenched tightly in a sweaty fist out of fear, procrastination, or laziness, is simply a waste. As you look at the seed that is your own life, which death will you choose?

Go to beaconhillbooks.com/go/nothingiswasted for a free downloadable study guide that includes questions for deeper personal reflection as well as activities for use in a small group setting.

9 ⟋ MELTING DOWN TO YOUR ESSENTIAL GOO

If you say the word *butterfly* to me, the first image that comes to mind is a cartoon butterfly, the kind you might see in a children's book. I picture a happy, sappy scene of pretty little creatures fluttering around the head of a Disney princess in a dazzling meadow.

I wish that were not the first image that comes to mind. Butterflies in my imagination are so connected to the realm of fairy tales and childhood that they seem more like fantasy creatures than what they really are—intricately designed, complex insects that taste with their feet, fly with delicate wings, and emerge into their butterfly form by the most astonishing method.

I want to see butterflies in a new way. Their beauty does not emerge easily. Like the seed that must fall to the ground and die to create the fruit-producing plant, butterflies also push their way out of a messy, deathlike state of destruction that is far harsher than I was taught in school.

Let's start with what I already knew about how a caterpillar becomes a butterfly. The caterpillar eats leaves until it achieves just the right weight that leads it to attach itself upside down to a twig or other object. Then it starts to produce a shell around

137

itself called a chrysalis. I witnessed this as a child when we used to catch caterpillars in bug catchers and shoeboxes and watch as these chrysalises formed.

That part of the process is impressive enough, but even more amazing is what happens next. It is hidden from view, so as I watched the chrysalis as a kid and waited for the butterfly to emerge, I never imagined the creative destruction that was taking place inside. As Ferris Jabr describes it in a *Scientific American* article, "First, the caterpillar digests itself, releasing enzymes to dissolve all of its tissues." Cut open the chrysalis during this process, he says, "and caterpillar soup would ooze out."[1]

Soup is certainly not what I have always pictured inside that chrysalis. I figured the caterpillar must be inside there growing wings and antennae and somehow changing its caterpillar self into its butterfly self. However, the caterpillar actually gets obliterated.

Molly Webster, a producer for the Radiolab *Black Box* hour heard on National Public Radio stations, visited the Florida Museum of Natural History to discuss the inside of the chrysalis with butterfly expert Andrei Sourakov.[2] To show her the process, he cut open a chrysalis that had been formed one day earlier. The caterpillar that had existed a day before was now nothing more than runny, pale goo that she said "looks like snot." Nothing in this gooey mixture looked anything like a caterpillar or a butterfly.

To anyone not familiar with this process, witnessing the goo stage would look like a complete disaster for the caterpillar. It has been wiped out of existence. There is also no obvious sign in this mess that *anything* living or useful, let alone something as intricate as a butterfly, would ever arise from this ugly stew. But just as the death or destruction of a planted seed is not the disaster it may appear to be but is, rather, a necessary step in the production of a plant, the caterpillar goo is also not the final word in the process of creating a butterfly. There is more to that goo than meets the eye.

What looks likes a soupy mess actually contains the building blocks of a beautiful creature. You can't get from caterpillar to butterfly without this stage of destruction. As Jabr explains, when the caterpillar is still inside its egg, it grows "imaginal discs" for each body part it will eventually need as a butterfly. Once the caterpillar disintegrates, the imaginal discs remain intact and use the goo as nutrients to grow the cells needed for various parts of the butterfly.[3] Out of seeming destruction, new life grows.

Just as the purpose of a seed is not to remain itself but rather to die in the ground and grow up as a plant, so the purpose of the caterpillar is to demolish its current self and become something entirely new, a butterfly. The caterpillar embodies that purpose not only from birth but even *before* birth, while it is inside its egg producing the imaginal discs. The destruction of the caterpillar is not an undermining of its purpose but a fulfillment of it. With some species of caterpillars, if you peel back the skin of the chrysalis and look inside, you can see some of the structures that will later become the wings, antennae, and other parts. Those structures are pushed up against the walls of the chrysalis and don't disintegrate into the goo.[4]

One question Molly Webster considers in her *Black Box* report on this process is, does the butterfly that emerges from this transformative destruction have the same *identity* as the caterpillar, or is it an entirely new creature? She interviewed Martha Weiss, a professor of biology at Georgetown University, who told of an experiment in which caterpillars were zapped each time they were exposed to a certain smell, which made them hate that smell. Then the caterpillars pupated, or went into the chrysalis stage, in which they disintegrated into the goo. The researchers wondered whether the moths that emerged would also hate the smell. Would the memory of that smell survive the goo? The moths did hate the smell, showing that, in a sense, the identity of the caterpillar survives the disintegration. The butterfly still has the memory of the caterpillar. They are the same creature, but transformed.

Although Webster was not presenting her report from a specifically Christian point of view, she was quick to see the spiritual analogies and implications of this process. The analogy she focuses on, as Christians have done for centuries, is how this process might relate to what happens to our bodies as they are resurrected in eternity. In what way is the person I will be in heaven, with a new body, still me?[5] If the caterpillar-butterfly transformation is any indication, my identity remains the same, but my body is new, glorified, entirely transformed.

Redemption Ain't Pretty

My identity in eternity is certainly worth pondering, but I am also intrigued by what implications this transformative process has for me here and now. What stands out most vividly to me about what happens to the caterpillar is how harsh the process is. As a kid, I pictured a more gentle, gradual transformation happening inside that chrysalis, with the caterpillar kind of asleep as it changed shape and grew wings and began to be a butterfly. But the complete *destruction* of the caterpillar? Reduced to sticky liquid? Does it have to be so messy? Isn't there a less violent way to get the job done? Can't the process be a little prettier, like the butterfly itself?

The truth is that, once that caterpillar is in the chrysalis, it is in the way. If its present form survived, it would serve no purpose. In order for that butterfly to be created, the caterpillar has to quit taking up all the space. There is not room for both of them, and since they are really the same creature, there can only be one or the other. This being survives either as a caterpillar or as a butterfly. It can't be both. If it *tried* to be both, or if somehow the process were interrupted in the middle without a full transformation, the result would be a disaster.

The caterpillar carries forward useful things that will be part of its new self, but those things—the pieces that will become wings, antennae, and so on—are useful *only* to the new self. They serve no purpose for the caterpillar. So the transformational method that now stands—messy and ugly though it may be—makes the most sense. It gets the job done.

Spiritual transformation can be just as painful, messy, and shattering as what happens to the caterpillar. Many of us, when faced with the need for spiritual change, try to make it happen by changing as little as possible. We want to become butterflies, but we also have grown fond of our caterpillar selves and would like to keep them intact for the most part. We fear and resist obliteration. We look for a compromise. We want to be both creatures.

When Jesus speaks of what is necessary for spiritual transformation, he rejects the "little bit of this and little bit of that" approach. You have to choose. Caterpillar or butterfly. You must be born again, Jesus tells Nicodemus in John 3. Isn't that what happens to the caterpillar? It was born once as a caterpillar, but to become what it was ultimately designed to be, it must be born again. It can't just attach a few wings to the old self. New birth from the goo is necessary.

Look how much Jesus demands from his disciples, how much he wants them to throw off everything about their old, caterpillar lives in order to be ready for him to change them into what he wants them to be. He knows it will be painful. He knows the personal cost for them will be great, and he tells them so. They will be hated, persecuted, shunned, misunderstood. In Matthew 10, for example, Jesus gives them instructions as he sends them out for ministry. It is not quite the pep talk they might wish for. It's all about stripping away things that will slow them down or divert them from their central purpose. As they go from town to town, healing people and preaching the message that the kingdom of heaven is near, they are not to acquire any gold, silver, or copper for their belts, and they are not to take any extra possessions with them. This will not be a money-making tour. They should stay with whatever villagers welcome them, and they should do their ministry and move on.

That plan, of course, assumes someone in the village *will* welcome them, but Jesus warns them that they are just as likely to be rejected. They can expect to be flogged in the synagogues, dragged before governors and kings, and called all kinds of nasty names, just as Jesus has been. Even their families are likely to turn against them.

Jesus strips away all illusions that forces such as wealth, popularity, or family connections will fuel their ministry. He dissolves his followers down to their essential, caterpillar goo. Near the end of this talk, he tells them, "Whoever finds their life will lose it, and whoever loses their life for my sake will find it" (Matthew 10:39). The caterpillar will be lost. But they should not fear or regret that. Something better is coming. The Father values them so much, Jesus tells them, that every hair on their heads is numbered. The process of spiritual transformation is painful, but it will be worth it in the end for those who endure. "Whoever acknowledges me before others," Jesus says, "I will also acknowledge before my Father in heaven" (Matthew 10:32).

Jesus's teaching reminds me of how often I stand in the way of my own spiritual transformation. Although part of his warning to his disciples has to do with opposition they will face from a hostile audience, his most adamant warnings have to do with opposition they will face from themselves—the desire for approval, the need for security, the longing for money, the tug of nostalgia for their old, familiar lives. They can't hang on to all that. All that will need to be melted away inside the chrysalis in order to make room for the butterfly. But don't worry, he urges them. Even though the natural tendency might be to fear this future, they shouldn't. The Father *knows* them. He loves them. He is looking out for them. He will guide them into a bright future, even though they will endure pain on the way there.

What It Looks Like to Hold On to the Old Self

When I say that Jesus's words to his disciples remind me of how often I block my own transformation, I think of many examples, big and small. For instance, right now I am struggling with thought patterns that interrupt my creative work. During times when I should be thinking about writing, I find myself wandering into these other issues instead. I am angry and frustrated about a dispute that is already settled and that I should have let go quite a while ago. But my mind wants to enter that battle again and again. I rehash arguments. I think of things I wish I had said. I construct little speeches I should have made. I envision new disputes and get angry as my mind plays out these scenarios even though they are entirely made up.

What do these interruptions do to my ability to sink deeply into my real work, the writing I need to do for that day? They destroy my concentration. Writing requires a delicate control of emotion and intellect, and pointless, angry daydreams are like a bomb going off in my brain, scattering thoughts in every direction.

It's easy for me to claim that I want to get rid of this anger, but if I am honest about it, my real desire is to hang on to it *and* get my writing done. I want to be able to switch back and forth effortlessly between the two. When I pray about my writing and this old grievance, I get a distinct impression from the Lord that my focus on this old dispute should simply die. It has no place in my brain anymore. It's part of the caterpillar life, and should be obliterated in the goo.

As you look at your own life, what part of your caterpillar existence needs to disintegrate to make room for the butterfly? If you are already a Christian, this process started when you turned your caterpillar self over to Christ at the time of conversion and asked him to do whatever it takes to make you a butterfly. When we surrender to Christ and ask for forgiveness of our sin that separates us from God, that sin gets obliterated in the gooey sea of God's forgetfulness, to bother us no more. But in one sense we remain in the goo our whole earthly lives as we grow in Christ, headed toward complete transformation in eternity.

One reason this ongoing change is so difficult is that, as caterpillars, it is often hard to picture what kind of butterfly we're supposed to become, and it's hard to see how God is going to get us there. At certain stages of the process, we see only goo. It often looks as if God has simply messed up. He melted too much of us away, and now we're in such a state of disintegration that it's hard to envision any way he could put us back together to make us even as good as we once were, let alone a new creature who will soar out of that chrysalis on wings. The chrysalis begins to feel more like a tomb than a workshop for building a beautiful, new creature. We look at our transformation-in-progress and think, *This is not where I thought God was going to take me. What's wrong with him? What is he doing?*

When a Shipwreck Helps You Reach Your True Calling

One woman I know who asked questions like that is Christin Taylor, who taught at my university and is the author of the book *Shipwrecked in L.A.: Finding Hope and Purpose When Your Dreams Crash*. Shipwreck is the metaphor Christin uses to describe something similar to the inside-the-chrysalis annihilation of the old self. It's a phenomenon I have seen repeated in the lives of numerous students over the years as they plan their lives in college then head out into the "real world." They move forward confidently, full of change-the-world, commencement-speech certitude about their futures. I have been in teaching long enough to see that these students often do change the world in significant ways but usually not in exactly the ways they expect. Sometimes it takes a shipwreck to lead them to their true callings.

For Christin Taylor, Hollywood was at the center of her bright dream. During her senior year at Indiana Wesleyan University, she spent a semester studying at the Los Angeles Film Studies Center. Through that experience, she got a good internship at Nickelodeon Movies. She loved her work there, which fueled her desire to work in the film industry and become, as she puts it, a "missionary to Hollywood."[6] After college, she and her husband, Dwayne, moved to Los Angeles, where he got a job and where Christin expected to get a job quickly in the entertainment industry she so loved.

She did all the right things, meeting with her internship contacts, visiting endless offices to drop off résumés, making follow-up phone calls. Nothing opened up. As a young couple living in an expensive city, she and Dwayne needed two incomes to make it. She had to find work.

Ironically, Christin's shipwreck turned out to be a job offer. She had sent out hundreds of résumés for film-industry jobs, but she applied for only one job outside the film industry. It was a position her husband had seen advertised in their church bulletin—administrative assistant to the youth ministry department. She didn't want the job. She thought getting stuck in that job would make it harder to pursue her Hollywood dreams. But with their shaky finances and no other prospects, she felt she had to apply. Even when they called her for an interview, she thought they would reject her once they saw that her real interests lay elsewhere.

After she got the job offer and accepted it, she went to her room and cried for three hours. She didn't *have* to take the job, of course, and the job itself didn't have to crush her film-industry dreams, but that was the effect this decision had on her. She felt that God's will must be for her not to work in the film industry, and if she ever did so, she would have to wait on his timing. Whatever that timing was, she felt certain it would not be soon. The death of this dream left her reeling, and she felt directionless and baffled. She was a blob of goo in her chrysalis.

Her crushed dream also made her feel that God had let her down. In *Shipwrecked in L.A.*, she writes, "In those days, I secretly felt a sense of betrayal and resentment that terrified me. Hadn't God called me to work in the film industry? Hadn't he opened the doors for us to move to Los Angeles, providing Dwayne a job? Why did he bring me all this way only to slam the door in my face?" Christin threw away all her job listings and contacts in the film industry. Rather than *ease* out of her job search, she brought her efforts to an abrupt halt, but that surrender "felt like amputating one of my limbs."[7]

There was no easy way out of Christin's dilemma. However, her pain was not wasted. As the months went by, she confronted issues she would have overlooked otherwise, such as anxiety that had plagued her for years. She writes, "As I embarked on my new role as the secretary for the youth ministries department at First Church, the anxiety that stirred my soul felt only like pain. Now I can see that it allowed me to finally deal with the things that had terrified me my whole life. Being lost freed me to find myself."[8]

Before she could find herself, however, she had to endure the frustration of a job that did not particularly value the creative skills that for so long had helped her define herself. In the church secretary position, she says she felt empty and blank. Although she doesn't make use of the caterpillar-butterfly image in her book, that blankness sounds like a perfect description of the goo stage. She was reduced to nothing, or seemingly nothing. Now it was time for the identity to build.

Several influences helped grow that new identity. One was a loving and innovative church called Mosaic, where Christin and her husband immediately felt welcome and where many in the congregation shared her love of creativity. The church, where the congregation sat in folding chairs on a dance floor and worshiped with loud music and were led by a charismatic pastor, had a much different style from what she had grown up with in Indiana. But she and her husband immediately felt at home.

As her faith was being revived at Mosaic, Christin also felt the desire to pursue a master's degree in creative writing. She enrolled at Antioch University. Although most of her fellow students were not Christians, her friendships with them helped build her faith because they pushed her to strip away aspects of her faith that were not living or thriving. She could not float along as a Christian with unchallenged beliefs. She was pushed out of her comfort zone and saw her faith with new eyes.

With these two strong influences working in her life, Christin's new identity began to emerge. Mosaic emphasized artistic ministries that focused on music, film, and other arts. It was here that she began to dip back into her interest in film. She was asked to work as a script supervisor on a short film for the church, which built her confidence and released a new sense of creativity. She says, "It was as if a dam was released. I was writing for school, but...ideas for short films, books, poems, and sketches began to pulse through me. Like trying to catch a passing fury, I could barely get all my ideas on paper, frantically scratching down images and dialogues in my journal or a scrap piece of napkin at a restaurant."[9]

As this creative work thrived, she finally felt free to shed one other aspect of her old identity, her church secretary job. She says she felt God standing over her, whispering, "It's okay, Christin. You don't have to stay anymore."[10]

When she left that job and looked for a new one, a friend told her that a film finance company in Beverly Hills was looking for an assistant. She applied for the job and got it. She said, "And just like that the doors that seemed to have slammed so tightly over my hidden dreams of working in the film industry for the last two years opened smoothly and silently on their hinges, inviting me in."[11]

Christin took this job and was finally working in the film industry as she had dreamed, but before long she realized that the identity into which she had grown did not really fit her old dream. This was not her world, and she didn't want to let it make her into someone she was not. She felt called to teaching at the college level, which is what she then pursued. Her shipwreck experience, then, was ultimately not about a postponed dream that she eventually was granted. It was an experience of transformation, shedding an old identity and taking on a new one, the one that was truly herself.

Is transformation really worth all the pain and disruption of having your entire being dissolved into a pool of muck inside the chrysalis? What if you're content being a caterpillar? Can't you simply hold on to that identity and let others go through the hassle of becoming butterflies if they so choose?

Nature doesn't offer that choice to the caterpillar, and life rarely offers that choice to us. The meltdown is going to happen. It's human nature to try to avoid pain, so most of us would wiggle out of this process if we could, but usually we don't even see it coming until we're already in the middle of it. The only choice we have is how we will respond. Christin Taylor grieved the loss of her earlier identity—and it was truly a loss—but then she groped her way toward an even better identity.

Go to beaconhillbooks.com/go/nothingiswasted for a free downloadable study guide that includes questions for deeper personal reflection as well as activities for use in a small group setting.

10 ✎ DIRT, MANURE, AND OTHER YUCKY THINGS

Dirt doesn't get much respect. Listen to the way people talk about it. Dirt is often equated with things that are bad. A corrupt politician is "dirty." An obscene movie is "dirty." If we want to find out something unflattering about someone, we "dig up dirt" about the person. A "dirtbag" is a contemptible person. Calling someone "as old as dirt" is not a compliment. One way to insult someone is to call him a "dirty dog" (that language also disrespects dogs, but that's another discussion). If someone is mean to you, the person is treating you "like dirt." If you are extremely poor, you are "dirt poor."

As a person who has lived my whole life in cities and suburbs, I usually take dirt for granted; or, when I am aware of it, I see it as a nuisance. If you asked me the first thing that pops into my mind when you say the word *dirt*, I think of what our dog tracks into the house in the morning after the sprinklers have created little patches of mud for her to run through. When I have to vacuum and clean her brown paw prints off the carpet, I am not grateful for dirt. Nor am I grateful for other, everyday appearances of dirt— the film of dirt that clings to my car or rests on my shoes or has to be dusted off the furniture. When I run or hike the dirt paths in the foothills near my home, I think of the dirt as something dead, a messier version of the asphalt streets I drive on.

That was my view until I started actually studying dirt. It's easy to find God's fingerprints on the beautiful parts of nature—rainbows, the Grand Canyon, flowers, majestic mountains, pristine sandy beaches. But what about lowly dirt, or—if we carry it even further—something as unloved as manure? What good can be found in things that stink? It's easy to see how someone could find hope in something like a rainbow, which is the very cliché of hope, but what about a mound of dirt or a pile of poop?

It didn't take me long to find people who adore dirt and believe manure is fabulous. William Bryant Logan's book *Dirt: The Ecstatic Skin of the Earth* and a documentary film called *Dirt! The Movie* made me a believer in the redemptive powers of both dirt and manure. After studying that book and watching that film, I will never look at those underappreciated substances the same way.

Where would we be without dirt?

Dead.

To some degree, of course, everybody understands that already. Dirt is the substance in which plants grow, making life possible for all living creatures, including human beings. Without the nourishment that comes from dirt, life on Earth would cease.

But Logan and other dirt experts show that dirt is far more lively and precious than we normally realize. It is not a lifeless mess. Dirt bursts with life and activity and diversity. In the *Dirt!* movie, Logan holds two handfuls of dirt toward the camera and declares, "This much soil probably has in it tens of billions of microorganisms." Anthropologist Jeremy Narby says, "A handful of terrestrial dirt contains more organized information than the surface of all the other known planets."[1]

All the bacteria and worms and microorganisms that inhabit the dirt are turning death into life. Redemption.

For dirt lovers, the smelly, messy process is beautiful. The documentary shows a compost pile that stands several feet high. It looks like a disgusting pile of garbage—bits of roots, weeds, old cucumbers, carrot pieces, leaves, stems, and various other bits of rotting garbage. The commentator in the film describes her pile in loving terms: "I really think of this compost pile as a giant casserole or, say, a lasagna because all these things are going to start cooking. That's the way compost works." When you combine the leaves and stems, the moist green materials like weeds, and the dried brown roots, etc., the "dried brown is the fuel, the moist green is the fire. When you add nitrogen and carbon together, you get this wonderful combustion, aided by our little friends the bacteria and the fungi that are in here making it all work. And it turns into something resembling the best soil you ever saw."[2]

From a pile of garbage comes life-giving soil.

Little did you know of the drama happening right under your feet. You kick a clod of dirt and think the crumbly brown pile is inert and lifeless, but where did that dirt come from? Lots of death is involved. Over the years—even centuries, and millennia—the dead leaves, dead branches, dead fungi, dead carcasses, bits of rock and other materials pile up on the ground. They are not wasted. They decompose and eventually become the top layer of soil called humus, which holds in water, nourishes the plants that grow in it, and allows for the whole cycle to keep repeating as new plants grow and die and eventually turn into life-giving dirt.

Dirt is all around us. Any of us could go out right now and scoop up a handful of it and be grateful for this hint of redemption that God has placed literally under our feet. But, like spiritual redemption, the hint of redemption buried in nature is easy to overlook. Many of us never give much thought to dirt one way or the other, even though we rely on it for our survival. As Nobel laureate and Green Belt Movement founder Wangari Maathai put it, "We think that diamonds are very important, gold is very important. We call them precious minerals. But they are all forms of the soil. But that part of this mineral that is on top, like it is the skin of the earth, that is the most precious..."[3]

If we gave dirt its due, our language would reflect its value. An expression like, "You have a heart of dirt" would sound just as complimentary as, "You have a heart of gold." Instead of negative sayings such as, "You treat me like dirt," we would say things like, "I love you like the dirt in my garden."

Why Should I Care?

Does any of this have implications for the redemption that matters most, the redemption of our souls? Nature repeatedly shows that we are not always in the reality that we think we are. The dirt under my feet is not what I thought it was. While it was doing its work to keep me alive, I was walking around on it with no appreciation or awareness at all. Many people miss the beauty of spiritual redemption in the same way. They're simply annoyed by any talk of it, or they think it doesn't apply to them, or they think of it in such a flawed or simplistic way that they reject it entirely.

Dirt is only one of countless aspects of nature in which life springs from death in ways that rarely penetrate my awareness. The mighty tree in my backyard exudes a sense of permanence and timelessness. It stands solid and majestic. It has been around longer than I have and looks as if it will be there long after I am gone. On any particular day, it looks static, but of course, that is the furthest thing from the truth.

That tree is in constant flux. The thousands of leaves change every year, and every other part of the tree—the branches, the trunk, the bark—is transforming second by second. I forget this, but the tree doesn't. All around me, nature is in constant, vibrant motion. To me it may look serene, but every aspect of the natural world around me is growing, dying, decaying, reproducing, moving, transforming. How many deaths do I witness every day in nature without realizing it? How often do I notice the new life that has sprung from death? I am the rather inattentive audience to a drama that never stops.

I like to take walks in the foothills above my home. I think of those peaceful trails through woods and streams as a contrast to the frenetic world of human activity I normally inhabit—the world of traffic to navigate, chores to complete, classes to teach, kids to pick up, deadlines to meet, emails to answer. When I take my walks, there is a reassuring sameness in all that I see, with those hills towering above me in their mute beauty exactly as they did a month or a year ago.

I forget, though, that the mountains are not at all the same as they were a year ago. The ground has shifted in ways imperceptible to my eyes. The foliage looks the same as it did a year earlier, but the grasses and weeds and flowers of a year ago have died and decomposed and been replaced by new growth. The gnats that annoy me today are not the same ones that bugged me a year ago. Those are all dead, replaced by new ones. I walk through a scene of immense slaughter. Thousands of insects, birds, squirrels, raccoons, and skunks are dead or dying all around me, even on days when I don't see a single one.

Nature doesn't waste all that death. Those dead animals feed other animals, or their carcasses decompose and create the soil that allows new plants to grow that will feed new generations of creatures. That's the silent backdrop to my peaceful hikes through the foothills. Nature sees no need to make a big display of this redemptive process. As it works out its quiet purposes, it also does not hesitate to use everything, even the lowliest materials, to create new life.

Which brings me to manure.

Why We Should Appreciate Poop

Even though the word *dirt* has a bad reputation and is used figuratively in negative ways, that is nothing compared to the contempt with which manure is treated. Think of all the impolite terms we have for poop. Think of the profanity that springs from it. Some of the terms are so bad that a polite publisher will not allow me to use them. And yet, manure is a beautiful thing.

In his book on dirt, Logan writes appreciatively of manure, and he is also careful to include urine in the mix because, "while the solid feces are comparatively rich in phosphorous, they contain only about one-third of the manure's nitrogen and one-fifth of its potash. The greater proportion of these two important nutrients is contained in the urine."[4] What can this smelly muck accomplish? It becomes food for a host of organisms that then become food for other creatures such as worms, mites, and beetles. All this feeding and breaking down of chemicals eventually transforms the whole messy concoction into rich, healthy soil.

Manure works wonders, but who is grateful for it? Before the automobile came along, when transportation depended more heavily on the horse, manure was a much bigger part of people's everyday lives. In the 1890s, New York City's horse population was approximately 175,000. Each horse produced about 30 pounds of dung a day, for a total of more than 5 million pounds of horse manure every day.[5] That was a big mess to deal with, of course, but it could have been a treasure. Think of all the good soil it could have created. What did people do with it? Spread it on farm fields? Cart it away for their gardens?

No. According to authors Frank Coffey and Joseph Layden, sanitation workers gathered it up each day, piled it on barges, and dumped it into the river. In other words, they turned it into pollution. By not understanding and not valuing the redemptive potential in all these tons of poop, they turned what might have been useful into something destructive.

Today, we do something similar. Logan says that cows, chickens, horses, sheep, and dogs create roughly two billion tons of manure annually, "enough for a three-foot layer over all the home gardens in America."[6] Great news! But less than one-fourth of it is returned to the soil in a useful way. Most of it gets hauled away at great expense and significant loss.

What the Dung Beetle Teaches about Redemption

Although people let their squeamishness about manure undercut its usefulness, one animal in particular does a better job of making the most of the dung that covers the earth, and the whole planet is better off because of it.

Just as manure is not on the list of favorite things for most people, beetles probably don't get too high a rating either. You may think of them as creatures that destroy gardens, ruin lawns, kill roses, and eviscerate forests. Fair enough. But consider one particular kind of beetle, the dung beetle, that loves manure so much she even lets her babies be born in it. As Logan explains, the dung beetle rolls the manure into smooth balls, then pushes it underground, where it will be safe from predators. Then she lays an egg inside it and tends to this dung ball until the little beetle is born.

Ancient Egyptians worshiped this beetle, which they called the scarab, and many amulets in the shape of this beetle survive to this day. Why did they hold the scarab in such high regard? "They revered it because it brought the dead to life," writes Logan. "The scarab was a symbol of eternal life."[7]

The beetle not only brings new life out of a ball of poop, but it also helps bring new life to the soil itself. Logan reports that the record number of scarabs on a single pile of elephant dung is around sixteen thousand! With all those beetles burrowing their precious bundles of dung into the dirt, the soil itself reaps the benefits. Nitrogen that would be lost if the dung remained above ground gets pushed into the dirt, where it can do some good. The buried manure also helps the soil retain more moisture, and improves aeration. That makes the grass grow better. "As a result," says Logan, "The herbivores are healthy and well fed. They defecate copiously. A cow is liable to leave fifteen patties per day; a single elephant turd weighs four pounds. The beetle is the linchpin of this cycle of renewal, which keeps a whole landscape healthy."[8]

Kill the Patient to Save His Life?

As I was knee-deep, metaphorically speaking, in my research on dirt and manure, I ran across a *New York Times* headline about a seemingly different subject altogether. The headline said, "Killing a Patient to Save His Life." I couldn't help but stop and read the article. Had they really found a way to save people by killing them?

The article described a new and controversial, experimental procedure that was about to be tried at an emergency room in a hospital in Pittsburgh. When trauma patients arrive with a gunshot or knife wound, doctors will drain out their blood and pump freezing saltwater in its place. As reporter Kate Murphy explains, "Without heartbeat and brain activity, the patients will be clinically dead."[9]

Before I go any further with the details of this, let me just say how crazy it sounds. Draining out someone's blood and replacing it with freezing saltwater? It sounds more like murder than rescue.

My first thought was to reject the blood-draining surgery idea even before I finished the article. But then I thought, *Everything I* have been writing over the last several chapters is actually just as un-expected and counterintuitive as killing a patient in order to save him. *Burying a seed to let it die so a plant can grow? Letting the caterpillar be dissolved in a blob of goo so a butterfly can take shape? Hearing a woman say that being hit by a car was the best thing that has ever happened to her?* I am getting used to reality not being structured the way I expect it to be. So when I hear that doctors want to kill people in order to save them, I keep an open mind.

If I were in charge of the universe, I would set it up so you simply *saved* someone in order to save them. I would leave out the killing part. But I am not in charge. And the universe is strange.

My own faith in Jesus Christ, for example, includes strange elements that I accept but don't fully understand. Violence is at the heart of Christianity. Jesus clearly taught that, in order for us to be saved, he had to die.

Why is reality set up so that salvation and other kinds of spiritual transformation are so often constructed out of pain? I wish it happened differently. Throughout this book, as I have told stories like Jerry Deans and the death of his daughter, or Amy Hauser suffering with breast cancer, I am happy for the spiritual transformation that came to them through these situations, but I also think, *Couldn't it have happened in an easier way?*

How does Jesus handle the excruciatingly painful part of the redemptive process? Does he readily accept it as necessary, or does he struggle and fight it, the way most of us do? A colleague at my university, biology professor Cahleen Shrier, has lectured on the intense physical pain suffered by Jesus during his crucifixion and the events leading up to it. She points out that crucifixion is "quite possibly the most painful death ever invented by humankind."[10] Before Jesus even reaches that horrible torture, however, he faces several rounds of other kinds of torments.

During the sleepless night before his execution, he walks about two and a half miles as he is taken to Pilate, to Herod, and back to Pilate. He is mocked, beaten, and flogged. Drawing on historical sources of the practices of that time, Shrier shows that Jesus would be flogged with a whip made of leather strips with metal balls attached to them, and a sheep bone at the end of each strip that would tear out chunks of flesh and expose the bone underneath. Jesus would lose a great amount of blood from this, and the pain would be intense.

The soldiers jam a crown of thorns on Jesus's head. As they puncture his skin, the thorns would damage the nerves of the face, causing terrible pain down his head and neck. By the time they are ready to crucify him, Jesus is probably in shock, thus unable to carry his cross.

Jesus would be thrown to the ground to be nailed to the cross, Shrier says. The wrists are included in the Greek meaning of "hands," so the nails may be driven through his wrists *or* hands. The nails, which are probably seven to nine inches long, would sever the major nerve to the hand. As if that were not painful enough, it becomes agonizingly worse once the cross is lifted and the full weight of his body hangs on those nails, ripping through the tissue of the hands and dislocating his shoulders and elbows. By that time the tops of his feet would already be nailed to the cross as well.

Hanging that way, with his body pulling down on his diaphragm, every breath he takes would be agony. He is slowly suffocating. Fluid builds up around his heart and lungs. Finally, he probably dies of a heart attack.[11]

Although we can ponder this horrendous physical pain, the inner agony that Jesus endures as a result of his separation from the Father is beyond human comprehension. When, in those last moments of life, he quotes from Psalm 22, "My God, my God, why have you forsaken me?," the depth of his sorrow must be worse than anything else he has endured.

Jesus Sought a Different Way Too

Despite all the time Jesus spent preparing his disciples for what was coming, as the moment approaches, Jesus himself looks for a different way to accomplish his mission. He cries out against it. He doesn't want to do it. As he prays in Gethsemane just before his betrayal and arrest, he tells his closest disciples, "My soul is overwhelmed with sorrow to the point of death" (Matthew 26:38). He falls facedown on the ground and prays, "My Father, if it is possible, may this cup be taken from me. Yet not as I will, but as you will" (Matthew 26:39). He goes back again later and asks the Father one more time to let the cup be taken away. He has brought his closest friends and disciples to keep watch with him, but they keep falling asleep. They are weak, but he still wants them there. He is in the depths of misery and wants all the support he can get, even if it is only from these flawed friends. A third time he goes to pray to the Father to find a different way.

As I look at Jesus's tormented prayers now, I find them immensely comforting. Even though no one in history ever had a clearer and more determined sense of mission than Jesus Christ, he still looks for a different way to accomplish it, one without all the agony and torment. He knows what must be done, and he is willing, but everything in him cries out against the method.

I find this comforting because, if even Jesus approaches his suffering with such reluctance, then who can blame any of us for crying out against the pain we must endure, even if we know that pain can lead to positive transformation? Explanations are one thing. Jesus knows the rationale for *why* he has to do what he is about to endure. He isn't making an *argument* against it. He is crying out against it.

When I look at almost all the stories of pain I have told in this book, I understand the *explanations* for how the pain was not wasted. I grasp, at an intellectual and spiritual level, how the process of transformation works. Still, none of that diminishes my distress over the pain itself. How grateful I am that the Bible records Jesus's similar sense of repugnance at the suffering. Being a follower of his does not mean denying one's anguish.

Every moment of Gethsemane shows me how to approach the times of dread. I learn from the fact that Jesus brings his friends with him. Not perfect friends, but men who really do love him, even though they're sleepy. In our darkest moments, some of us feel tempted to close ourselves off and hunker down alone, but Jesus shows that people who care about us—even if there isn't much they can do—make a big difference in pulling us through those times.

Jesus also shows persistence in his prayers. He approaches the Father three times with the same prayer. There is nothing wrong with that. If it's on your mind, bring it to God. If it *stays* on your mind, bring it back to God. Unlike Jesus's companions, the Father is never sleepy. You can pour out your agony to him all you want.

The "not as I will, but as you will" part of Jesus's prayer teaches me something important. Jesus pours out his agony and looks for a way out of it, but ultimately, he trusts in the Father's will and plan. As a follower of Christ, I am grateful that I have the freedom to say, *I don't get this, Lord. I wouldn't do it this way. It looks like a mistake. It looks unnecessarily harsh.* Sometimes God does show me a way out. He answers my prayer by bringing relief—a change of circumstances, a person sent to help, or a miracle. But if he doesn't do that, then being his follower means saying, as Jesus did, *I won't run from you. I won't turn my back on what you have put before me. I won't insist on waiting until my finite knowledge and limited perspective bring me complete understanding. Your will be done. I move forward with you.*

After his agonizing prayer at Gethsemane, Jesus faces what happens next with courage and determination. In doing so, he changes the course of history.

You're Going to Do *What* to that Gunshot Victim?

Which brings me back to the *New York Times* story about the experiment in which the doctors are going to kill the patient in order to save the patient. Imagine that you are wheeled into the emergency room with a gunshot or knife wound. What would you say if they told you the first step in your treatment was going to be to drain all your blood and replace it with freezing saltwater, which would halt your heartbeat and suspend your brain activity? Would you jump at this chance? Or would you insist on being taken to another hospital immediately?

Actually, the patients who have this procedure won't even be given a choice. They will already be unconscious because of the severity of their injuries. The hospital doing the procedure is offering bracelets to anyone who wants to opt out of this experiment now, just in case they should ever end up in this life-threatening situation, but few people anticipate such a specific catastrophe for themselves.

Why would doctors perform a surgery that, at first glance, looks so destructive? Simply put, it buys them time. The procedure will be used only with patients whose injuries are so severe that they have gone into cardiac arrest because of blood loss. Usually with these kinds of patients, doctors have only about five minutes to restore blood flow and avoid brain damage. Less than 10 percent of these patients survive. The new procedure, if it works, should give doctors up to an hour to work on a patient's injuries before brain damage occurs. People can survive on little oxygen if their body is cold. Flushing this cold solution into the patient's body will reduce body temperature to 50 degrees Fahrenheit, and afterward the body will gradually warm as the blood is put back in. The heart should start beating again once the body temperature reaches 85 to 90 degrees. It may take several hours, or even days, for the patient to regain consciousness.[12]

If you find this whole idea outlandish, you are not alone. Dr. Thomas M. Scalea, a trauma specialist, is quoted as saying, "This is 'Star Wars' stuff. If you told people we would be doing this a few years ago, they'd tell you to stop smoking whatever you're smoking, because you've clearly lost your mind."[13] The surgery obviously contains many risks. Can the patient really be brought back to life after such a radical procedure? Will the brain be damaged? Is this ethical?

Those are valid questions, but the alternative is almost certain death. That's why proponents say the surgery is worth the chance. It induces death, but the death is not wasted. The death is the only chance for life.

Sound familiar? Jesus's death is the same way. It is horrible, disgusting, and painful even to think about, but it is our only chance for life. Jesus knew it. He was willing to go through it because he knew resurrection would follow. He knew it would not be wasted. He knew we would benefit for eternity.

Jesus asked that the cup be taken from him. How many times have you asked the Father a similar question? *Please, Lord, not this. There must be another way. Please don't make me face this.*

Sometimes there is *not* another way. Sometimes the only path to life is through death. We will not have to travel that path alone. We can walk it with One who understands it better than anyone else ever will.

Go to beaconhillbooks.com/go/nothingiswasted for a free downloadable study guide that includes questions for deeper personal reflection as well as activities for use in a small group setting.

11 ✺ DOING LAUNDRY FOR 10,000 YEARS?

Where is your life headed?

If someone were to ask you that question, a reasonable but rather cynical-sounding answer might be death. That really is where every life is headed.

I know my own death could happen at any time. I have had a whole lifetime to think about this and prepare for it, but if I died today, I have to admit I would be surprised. Any time someone I know dies, I also feel the sting of disbelief, even if the person was gravely ill.

Although I am aware of the reality of death, I do not shape my dreams and plans according to that inevitable fact as much as the looming reality of it might indicate that I should. On an everyday basis, death doesn't feel as real as other realities.

Plans I am making for next year seem real. The work that needs to be done on the house feels real. Chores that need to be completed at work feel real. The tasks I need to carry out to take care of my kids feel real. The list of what feels real is long, but death is not on it, unless I take time to really concentrate on it, which is rare.

On most days, I'm not trying to defeat death, which is not really on my mind; rather, I am trying to reach that point of smoothing out my life in a way that makes it have a sense of *completeness*, a sense in which I could say, *Now* everything is in place. *Now* things are the way I want them to be with my work, my relationships, my spiritual life, my health, my future. Now I can coast along on this reality, enjoying each day, my worries abolished.

I never reach that point, of course. No one does. It is illusory, and even if I were to achieve this ideal state at some point, I would do so knowing it couldn't last long. Something would be bound to go haywire before long, and even if it didn't, death would eventually bring it all to a screeching halt.

Completeness is the unspoken ideal to which I am naturally drawn. For me, it often seems as if I am about six months from achieving that state. (However, a countervailing force inside me, which is most likely to assert itself when I wake up suddenly in the middle of the night, contradictorily tempts me to believe that complete disaster awaits in about that same six-month time period.)

Why this strange desire for completeness? Why don't I give it up since, deep down, I know it won't arrive? In the best moments of life, I almost think I achieve it. It's hard to describe those moments of perfection, of ecstasy, when I think, *This is it. This is what I am after.* If you search your own life, maybe you know the kind of perfect moments I am referring to, a fleeting state of being that hints at something better than this life, beyond it. You can *almost* grasp it and make it yours but not quite, not for long. I have sensed these moments—which I think of as hints of eternity—in certain pieces of music, in times of deep worship when God's presence comes especially close, in certain times of prayer, in a few encounters with God's Spirit in the majesty of nature, in a few times of deep connection with another person, and in certain powerful moments in novels and films.

Others have written about these moments of perfection and longing. In *The Weight of Glory*, C.S. Lewis writes of the "inconsolable secret" that "pierces with such sweetness that when, in very intimate conversation, the mention of it becomes imminent, we grow awkward and affect to laugh at ourselves; the secret we cannot hide and cannot tell, though we desire to do both."[1] Sometimes the secret is simply called beauty, but that doesn't fully grasp the reality of it. Sometimes it is associated with nostalgia for a moment in one's past, but it is really not located in the past. Sometimes the beauty is thought to reside in the works of music, art, or literature through which we experienced it, but as Lewis says,

> The books or music in which we thought the beauty was located will betray us if we trust to them; it was not in them, it only came through them, and what came through them was longing. These things—the beauty, the memory of our own past—are good images of what we really desire; but if they are mistaken for the thing itself, they turn into dumb idols, breaking the hearts of their worshippers. For they are not the thing itself; they are only the scent of a flower we have not found, the echo of a tune we have not heard, news from a country we have not yet visited.[2]

Life's harsher and more mundane realities easily extinguish these brushes with moments of completeness. We have work to do, chores to complete, problems to solve. The longing that, in the perfect moment, rises to the surface and is almost fulfilled now fades into the distance. It doesn't disappear. We still yearn, we still push toward that state of being at which the moments of beauty have hinted.

Life always runs out before we reach it. Is the problem that life is too short and too beset with complications and difficulties? We get sick, we get old, we die in the middle of our search. What would happen if we could smooth out those difficulties and produce a life that was much longer, much healthier, much more subject to our personal control? Would we then find what we are looking for?

What If I Had a Few Extra Millennia to Work With?

When I was a teenager, I thought the landscape of life looked something like this:

• First there is childhood, where you learn the basics—talking, walking, getting along with people, stuff like that.

• Then come the teenage years, full of turmoil and adventure, deciding who you'll become, what you'll do, whom you'll date. These are the years when people are most alive, I thought, and when the most important things happen.

• Then comes college and its aftermath, up to about the mid-twenties, when you finish your education, choose a career, probably find a spouse, settle into a community and job, turn into an adult.

• After that, I envisioned what I thought of as the coasting years, when you live the usual adult existence of work, home, kids, and an occasional vacation or two. I thought of this time as a little predictable, a little dull, but fairly easy. You just do the same things over and over. I thought this era of life stretched on for an *extremely* long time, forty or fifty years, which might as well have been eternity in my mind.

• Finally, there would be a short period of creaky old age, followed by death.

Imagine my surprise when I reached adulthood and discovered that *there are no coasting years.* Every era of life is filled with disruptions, challenges, losses, thrills, dangers, disappointments, fulfillments.

Like many teenagers, I looked at my parents' lives and thought they had pretty much achieved what they sought from life and were now simply gliding contentedly through the rest of it until old age hit them. That was an illusion. I now understand that, even though their lives were satisfying in many ways, they still had the same kinds of longings, complaints, and unfulfilled dreams that I now have as a father of teenagers.

As a teenager, I figured most old people understood that life was just about over for them, and they were ready to contentedly accept their fate. I now realize that most of them want more time, even when their lives are difficult. Even after all those decades, they still have not achieved the completeness they sought.

What if they, and all the rest of us, did have more time? What if, instead of a life span of eighty years or so, we had a thousand years to work with, or several times that? Would the fulfillment that so eludes us in this short life finally come?

Scientists, entrepreneurs, and visionaries are working toward the goal of a dramatically extended life span for human beings. Others take the idea further, reimagining what it even *means* to be human. Are our physical bodies, for example, an essential part of our identity as humans, or is the true self merely the patterns of information that reside in the brain? What if we could separate that self from the relatively frail, constantly aging mortal body in which it is housed? What if we could place that self into a different, longer-lasting container? If that self could be taken out of the body and stored in a computer, could we make backup copies of ourselves and essentially become immortal?[3]

Those questions, which sound like something from science fiction, are currently being pursued by scientists and thinkers from various fields. Other efforts are underway to dramatically slow the aging process and make the physical body itself last far longer than it does now. In an article called "The Methusaleh Manifesto," Ronald Bailey reports on a longevity summit in 2009 in which scientists and other experts gathered to find a way to make "extreme human life extension" possible within the next twenty years or so. His article begins, "If you're under age 30, it is likely that you will be able to live as long as you want. That is, barring accidents and wars, you have centuries of healthy life ahead of you."[4] *Centuries* of life ahead for people already living now? How could that be possible?

These futuristic thinkers put their faith in a concept they call "longevity escape velocity," meaning that the closer you get to the year that you would expect to die under the current life expectancy, the further new technologies will push that death date away. Futurist Ray Kurzwell told the longevity summit participants, "We are very close to the tipping point in human longevity. We are about 15 years away from adding more than one year of longevity per year to remaining life expectancy... Health and medicine will be a million times more powerful in 20 years."[5] These thinkers anticipate not just *steady* growth in anti-aging technology over the next two decades but *exponential* growth, similar to the growth in computer technology over the last few decades.

Bailey's article cites dramatic strides in longevity research that has already been done in animals. Biologist Michael Rose of the University of California-Irvine has done work that has produced fruit flies that live four times longer than normal, giving them life spans that are the human equivalent of three hundred years.

Significant scientific barriers still stand in the way of fulfilling this vision of near immortality for humans. But to those at the longevity summit, the progress so far has been so impressive and the rewards of a thousand-year life span are so enticing that they can't understand why more people aren't thrilled about it. Bailey wrote, "Hanging over the entire event was a single question: Why are so many people unaware of the tantalizing possibility of soon achieving extreme human life extension? And why do so many reject it when they hear about it?"[6]

Why Is a Thousand Years Not Enough?

One answer the summiteers at the longevity conference offered about the lack of enthusiasm for an extreme life span increase is that many people find the idea of living for hundreds of years creepy. Another problem is that people don't yet trust the idea of extreme human life extension because it reeks too much of a scam. They discussed the possibility of enlisting celebrities to help persuade the public of the legitimacy and benefits of this movement. They also have been surprised that no billionaire with a desire for a personal life extension of a few hundred years has stepped up to fund the research that might speed up the process of achieving near immortality.[7]

Creepiness and lack of celebrity endorsements and billionaire funding may be part of the reason extreme human life extension has not caught on as quickly as its proponents would like, but I suspect something deeper is behind people's reluctance to fully embrace this promise of long life. I personally want to live forever, and as a Christian, eternal life is my hope and expectation. But I don't want to live forever in life *as it is now*. I wouldn't want to live forever in this life, even if all aging and illnesses and disabilities were removed. I want something more.

If I were merely given a few hundred or thousand more years of life as it is now, I believe the things I now love would get old, the things I now tolerate I would end up hating, and the things I now hate would become unbearable. For example, right now I love my job teaching, but would I still love it 653 years from now? How would I feel when I was still grading papers in my 974th semester? How much would I enjoy marking comma splices for literally the billionth time? Even though I rarely acknowledge it, one of the reasons I treasure teaching so much now is that I know it will eventually come to an end. My career is flying by quickly, so

I want to value it while it lasts. If I knew that I still had hundreds of years left to go, would it feel like such a gift?

Why not simply retire from work after 150 years or so of this thousand-year life and have fun for the final 850 years? That sounds promising at first, but how would I pay for this long retirement? Maybe I could cycle through several different careers, spending a hundred or so years in each of them until I got bored and moved on to something else. How many jobs would I really want to do?

The idea of this extremely long life is already making me feel tired. And so far I have only considered the implications for work. What about all the other aspects of life that may be tolerable for eighty or ninety years but that would grow more tedious as the centuries wore on? How many thousands of times do you really want to trim those hedges or unclog those drains or wash those loads of laundry or clean the carpet or change the oil in the car, or the next car, or the dozens of cars after that? Would those things become more enjoyable over time, or less?

Some might ask, *But is this extension of human life really all that different from what Christians say they long for, eternity in heaven? Won't that get tedious too, since it will last not only for a thousand years but tens of thousands of years and beyond?*

Unfortunately, the popular conception of heaven often makes it look far worse than simply a thousand years tacked on to our current life. If it were all about floating around on clouds and playing harps, then count me out. However, that false stereotype of eternity has nothing to do with the reality toward which we are headed. Here is the reality: Eternity is the *fulfillment* of the good things our earthly life promises but never quite delivers. It is not simply *more* of what we have now; it is a life of an entirely different character.

Why Is Eternity so Hard to Imagine?

If eternal life is so great, then why has it been reduced to a set of clichés that make so many of us prefer our current lives? The problem lies in the limitations of our imaginations, not in the limitations of the reality.

It reminds me of the limitations a child has in imagining what it will be like to be an adult. When I was a kid, I imagined a very different adulthood from what I now have or from what I would now want. I thought adulthood was all about freedom to do whatever I wanted. I would finally be free from the stifling and unnecessary restrictions my parents always placed on me, and I intended to exploit that freedom in every way imaginable. I loved roller coasters as a kid, but I got to ride them only once or twice a year because my parents wouldn't take me to the big theme parks more often than that. I decided that when I grew up, I would spend every day possible riding roller coasters! I had a vague sense that I would have to work to pay for things, but I was determined that every day I wasn't working, I would be headed to a roller coaster.

I liked milkshakes also, but my parents limited how many I could drink. I planned to lift those restrictions as an adult. I also planned to abolish restrictions on staying up late, eating piles of M&Ms, turning off lights to save electricity, doing chores, keeping the music volume low, and a long list of other oppressive mandates. I could hardly wait!

My actual adult life bears little resemblance to that childhood vision, even though I could fulfill much of it if I really wanted to. Roller coasters are still fun, but they are no longer at the top of my list of most enjoyable activities. I'm now happy to consume M&Ms and milkshakes in moderation. On most days I would prefer the chance to go to bed a little early rather than have to stay up even later. I enjoy things now that wouldn't have occurred to me to want as a child. The books I now love to read would have been dull or incomprehensible to my child self. The teaching duties that now give me such satisfaction would have looked like nothing but onerous obligations when I was a kid. A steaming cup of coffee or a quiet evening at home after a long week are treats to me now but would have been useless to me then. And the list goes on.

If we cannot truly grasp adulthood while we are living in childhood, even though the two states of being are separated by a relatively small number of years and contain many shared experiences, then how can we expect to grasp eternity while we live in mortality, since the two states of being are separated by a far wider gulf and are of entirely different realms of experience? As Lewis points out, "Heaven is, by definition, outside our experience, but all intelligible descriptions must be of things within our experience."[8] The biblical authors who describe heaven must use mostly symbolic language to suggest the majesty of heaven—streets of gold, walls of jasper, gates of pearl, and so on. If jewels don't mean much to you, then you might read these descriptions of heaven and think, *Big deal. I'd rather just stick to my own life for a few hundred more years.*

More of the Same, or a Leap into the Unknown?

A heavily jeweled landscape is not the point, of course. The point is that the reality of this new realm is so different from anything we have experienced that it's impossible for us to truly understand it in our current life. Throughout this book, we have seen this same principle at work. If you had never seen a plant or tree, for instance, it would be hard to imagine such a concept by simply looking at a *seed* from which such a thing would spring. If you *were* a seed, you might prefer to simply remain that way forever rather than risk being planted and destroyed in order to become something you don't fully comprehend. You might support a movement that promised longer life for seeds. The same is true if you were a caterpillar. If you had never seen a butterfly, you might simply prefer to extend your caterpillar life indefinitely rather than trade it for some unknown transformation.

Human beings cannot fully grasp the significance of the Bible's promise of eternal life. But that doesn't mean we are incapable of knowing *anything* about it. We have that longing. Those hints of something beyond us. Those moments of connection when we can *almost* know it. If we pay attention to these hints (and it's easy to live in such a way that we completely miss them), then we realize that this new place, hazy though it seems to our limited understanding, is our true home. "We do not want merely to *see* beauty," writes Lewis, "though, God knows, even that is bounty enough. We want something else which can hardly be put into words—to be united with the beauty we see, to pass into it, to receive it into ourselves, to bathe in it, to become part of it."[9]

Our relatively short life span here, which so often feels *too* tragically short since we reach the end of our lives still wanting *more*, is redeemed by the fulfillment of eternity. We will never find the *more* that we truly desire in this life simply by adding a hundred or ten thousand years to our life span. What we seek is somewhere else.

There are times, however, when it would be very hard to convince me that what I really want is in eternity. There are times when I would be willing to trade the vague promise of a "union with beauty" or an intimate and eternal connection with God for the thing that I see right before me that I am dying to have. In those moments I know what I want, and it's here and now.

My house is littered with the discarded remnants of these urgent desires that my children thought would satisfy them over the years as they grew up. I can't count the number of times they came to my wife and me to beg for the one thing that would fulfill their deepest longings. They promised that if we would just get them *this*, they would not ask for anything else. Why would they need to? *This* would satisfy them. Now the paintball guns and masks, toy cars, dolls, video game consoles, bats, gloves, bicycles, half-read books, and many other remnants of those ultimate desires either litter a corner of the garage or were long ago given away so some other child could fulfill those same urgent yearnings.

My wife and I were happy to buy our kids all that stuff when we could. They learned from all of it and enjoyed it. We knew it wouldn't be the last thing they wanted. We knew their desires would wear out before the equipment itself did. That's how earthly desire works. It's easy to see it in children, but it's harder to see it as adults, with the things we yearn for. For us, it really does seem as if certain things would be all we need. We may spend our whole lives trying to grasp that thing. For some, a particular person to love seems like the answer. For others, a particular career, or a certain level of wealth, or a certain degree of fame seems like the thing that will satisfy them. Some people have only vague ideas about this desired thing, but some people can name it precisely. I knew a man who went all over the world in the military, but what he really wanted—what he thought would satisfy him—was to retire to the hometown where he had grown up. After twenty years he did so, but the town he thought he was returning to wasn't really there anymore. It had changed so much that he could have picked almost any American town.

Many of these lifelong yearnings may bring a certain measure of contentment, but it is always limited. Ultimate purpose and fulfillment do not reside in this life. No added length of time will change that. No fine-tuning of a desire will overcome it. We were built for this earth, but we were also built for eternity. Squeezing everything we can out of this life brings joy, but so does letting go of it at the proper time.

Listening for the Faint Music of Eternity

God has "set eternity in the human heart," says the author of Ecclesiastes (3:11). We were built for it. We long for it, even when we don't identify it as the thing toward which we yearn. Jesus, Paul, and other wise figures in Scripture were good at balancing their commitment to this life with their ultimate tie to the next one.

Most people, if asked whether they would prefer to be alive or dead, would quickly choose life. But chained up in prison and writing a letter to the church at Philippi, Paul tells them he can't decide which he prefers: life or death. "For to me, to live is Christ and to die is gain," he told them. "If I am to go on living in the body, this will mean fruitful labor for me. Yet what shall I choose? I do not know! I am torn between the two: I desire to depart and be with Christ, which is better by far; but it is more necessary for you that I remain in the body" (Philippians 1:21-24). His ambivalence has nothing to do with the fact that he is suffering in prison and would like to end that. In fact, he says that his time in prison has served to advance the gospel because the whole palace guard is now aware that he is in chains for Christ, and other Christians are now more daring in their own stance for Christ. His pain is being redeemed, and the cause for which he lives is being advanced. So there are reasons to cling to life, but there are also reasons to let it go.

Jesus also pushed his followers to live life to the fullest—loving God and serving others—but not to invest their hope in this life. In Matthew 6 he urges them to hold on lightly to the things of this life. "Do not store up for yourselves treasures on earth," he tells them, "where moths and vermin destroy, and where thieves break in and steal. But store up for yourselves treasures in heaven, where moths and vermin do not destroy, and where thieves do not break in and steal. For where your treasure is, there your heart will be also" (6:19-21). Jesus and Paul are both fully engaged in life here and now—if they weren't, we wouldn't still be reading and talking about them—but they also live fully aware that this life is quickly passing away and that eternity is so close you can almost touch it.

Although both Jesus and Paul show how death is redeemed, that does not minimize how horrible death itself is. As I consider my own coming death, I dread the event itself. I hate to think of the pain that may precede it. Will it come after years ravaged by illness and the decline of old age? Or will it hit me in one horrifying, catastrophic moment? As I brace for my own end, I also mourn those I have lost to death. I brace myself for the inevitable grief that will hit me again as other friends and loved ones die. It is true that death is a passage into eternity, but that corridor is not clean and bright. It is filled with suffering—hospitals, IV tubes, confusion, pain, fear, loss of freedom, humiliation. As it ends one life, it disrupts countless others around it.

Death is an enemy, but it is not wasted. It will fall away. Hope shines through it. A beautiful country lies beyond. Earlier I wrote of Jesus's tremendous agony in Gethsemane as he contemplates his pending death, and then his excruciating torment during the crucifixion itself. Throughout his life he knows what is coming. As he prays to the Father to let the cup pass from him, he doesn't try to minimize how terrible it is going to be. As he ministers with his disciples, he does not live in denial of the agony that awaits him. But he also does not let anticipation of his own death crush hope, either his own or that of his followers.

As he shares his final meal with his disciples—with his arrest, torture, and crucifixion mere hours away—Jesus still is able to say to these followers, "Do not let your hearts be troubled" (John 14:1a). That is the opposite of what you might expect him to say. They have every reason to be troubled. Their leader is about to be taken away from them and brutally killed. Jesus dreads his own death, but he also is looking beyond it, and he wants them to grasp a vision for what happens next also. He adds, "You believe in God; believe also in me. My Father's house has many rooms; if that were not so, would I have told you that I am going there to prepare a place for you? And if I go and prepare a place for you, I will come back and take you to be with me that you also may be where I am" (John 14:1b-3). Even during the worst twenty-four hours of his life, Jesus pushes toward hope. It is not an empty sentiment. He knows that what he will prepare for his followers in eternity will far outweigh the pain that he and they are about to suffer, as hard as that may be to believe during the hours it is happening.

In my own darkest moments, I have trouble focusing on anything but the dreadful circumstances in which I am wallowing. Occasionally, though, even in those bad times, maybe *especially* during those bad times, I get a hint of the joy that is to come. For reasons that completely defy everything I see in front of me, I feel a lightness, a stomach-fluttering anticipation, about the future that awaits. It is similar to what sometimes happens when I eagerly await a far-off trip. In the midst of a difficult day, I might suddenly picture myself in that vacation spot where I'm going. I almost feel the sand between my toes, almost hear the waves swooshing onto the shore, almost feel the warmth of the sun on my face.

Eternity is like that. It is distant, but occasionally I hear the faintest burst of its music. I feel a jolt of the happiness that is to come. *Do not let your hearts be troubled,* Jesus says. *I am going to prepare a place for you.*

Do you hear the music? Are you listening for it?

Go to beaconhillbooks.com/go/nothingiswasted for a free downloadable study guide that includes questions for deeper personal reflection as well as activities for use in a small group setting.

ACKNOWLEDGMENTS

I am grateful for all the help and encouragement that flowed my way during the writing of this book. There is not room to thank everyone who deserves it, but I would like to give special appreciation to a few people by name.

I would like to thank those who allowed me to tell parts of their stories in this book or who provided other helpful content: Jerry Deans, Jerry Sittser, Amie Longmire, Amy Hauser, Jim Davis, Kathleen Anderson, Sandi Welborn, and Christin Taylor.

My colleagues, students, and supervisors at Azusa Pacific University are a consistent source of help and encouragement. The university has valued my writing and has allowed me to fit it into my schedule. I would like to thank my department chair, David Esselstrom; deans David Weeks and Jennifer Walsh; vice provost Vicky Bowden, and provost Mark Stanton. Two of my student assistants, Jeremy Verke and Lianna Moneypenny, were particularly helpful in carrying out various tasks related to this book.

I don't know how I would manage to finish a book without the prayer support of my Christian writers and artists group, the Ninos. They prayed for this book from the idea stage to the completed manuscript. I also would like to thank my church, especially the Spectrum class, for their spiritual inspiration and influence. I am grateful for the leadership of our pastor, Mike Platter.

Steve Laube is an outstanding agent who has given me wise advice and unfailing support. I am thankful for him. I also would like to express my gratitude to Bonnie Perry and the staff of Beacon Hill Press, publisher of five of my books, for giving me the chance to write about these ideas that are so important to me.

My wife, Peggy, and my children, Jacob and Katie, deserve a huge thanks for putting up with me during the writing of this book. They have been patient and loving during my many hours of work. I love them dearly and feel so fortunate to be husband and father to them.

NOTES

Chapter 1

1. "History of Enterprise." *http://www.enterpriseal.gov/#!history-of-enterprise/c6gw*. Last accessed October 2, 2015.

2. Ibid.

3. Kim Fulton-Bennett. "Fishing out the life histories of dead whales." Press release for the Monterey Bay Aquarium Research Institute, December 6, 2010.

4. Ibid.

5. C.S. Lewis, *Mere Christianity* (San Francisco: HarperSanFrancisco, 2001), 55-56.

Chapter 2

1. Kathleen Anderson, "From Powerlifter to Powerless," *Christianity Today*, May 25, 2012, *http://www.christianitytoday.com/ct/2012/may/powerlifter-to-powerless.html*. Last accessed October 2, 2015.

2. Ibid.

3. Ibid.

4. Jerry Sittser, *A Grace Revealed: How God Redeems the Story of Your Life* (Grand Rapids: Zondervan, 2012), 81.

5. Ibid.

6. Ibid., 68-69.

7. Ibid., 184.

8. Ibid., 185.

9. Ibid., 23.

10. Anderson, "From Powerlifter to Powerless."

11. Sittser, *A Grace Revealed*, 184.

12. Karen O'Connor, "Surprised by Redemption: How Trouble Can Transform Marriage," *Today's Christian Woman*, September 5, 2012, *http://www.todayschristianwoman.com/site/utilities/print.html?type=article&id=98335*. Last accessed October 2, 2015.

Chapter 3

1. Amy K. Hauser, *In His Grip: A Walk through Breast Cancer* (Indianapolis: WestBow Press, 2012), 6.

2. Ibid., 20-21.

3. Ibid., 119.

4. Ibid., 29-30.

5. Ibid., xxiii.

6. Ibid.

Chapter 6

1. Jonathan Gottschall, *The Storytelling Animal: How Stories Make Us Human* (Boston: Mariner Books, 2013), 48.

2. Ibid., 49.

3. Ibid., 43-44.

4. Ibid., 33.

5. Ibid., 52.

6. Christian R. Davis, *Reading for Redemption: Practical Christian Criticism* (Eugene, OR: Wipf & Stock, 2011), 12.

7. Ibid., 7.

8. Mark Twain, *The Adventures of Huckleberry Finn*, in *The Norton Anthology of American Literature*, Vol. C, Ed. Nina Baym (New York: Norton, 2012), 262.

9. Alissa Wilkinson, "It's the End of the World (At Least At the Movies)," *Christianity Today*, June 26, 2013. *http://www.christianitytoday.com/ct/channel /utilities/print.html?type=article&id=110705*. Last accessed October 6, 2015.

10. Joy Bassardet, "Will Smith Saves the World Again, and Again, and Again," *Unreality Magazine*, June 4, 2013. *http://unrealitymag.com/index .php/2013/06/04/will-smith-saves-the-world-again-and-again-and-again/*. Last accessed October 6, 2015.

11. Jordan Crucchiola, "How Many Times Has Will Smith's Family Saved the World? A Handy Chart," *Wired*, May 31, 2013. *http://www.wired .com/underwire/2013/05/ul_censussmiths/*. Last accessed October 6, 2015.

12. "Jesus: More than Our Super Man." *http://ministry-resources.s3 .amazonaws.com/man-of-steel/Jesus-more-than-our-superman.pdf*. Last accessed October 6, 2015.

13. John Steinbeck, *The Grapes of Wrath* (New York: Penguin, 2002), 386.

14. Ernest Hemingway, *The Old Man and the Sea* (New York: Scribner, 1995).

15. C.S. Lewis, "Myth Became Fact," *God in the Dock: Essays on Theology and Ethics* (Grand Rapids: Eerdmans, 1970), 66-67.

16. C.S. Lewis, "Answers to Questions on Christianity," *God in the Dock: Essays on Theology and Ethics* (Grand Rapids: Eerdmans, 1970), 57-58.

17. C.S. Lewis, *Surprised by Joy: The Shape of My Early Life* (New York: Harcourt, Brace and Co., 1955), 216, 223-224, 235-237.

18. Ibid., 191.

Chapter 7

1. Richard Stern, quoted in Mihaly Csikszentmihalyi, *Creativity: Flow and The Psychology of Discovery and Invention* (New York: Harper Perennial, 1997), 260.

2. Gyorgy Faludy, quoted in Mihaly Csikszentmihalyi, *Creativity: Flow and The Psychology of Discovery and Invention* (New York: Harper Perennial, 1997), 84.

3. John Updike, *Self-Consciousness: Memoirs* (New York: Fawcett Crest, 1989), 42.

4. Ibid., 48.

5. Ibid., 76.

6. Ibid., 83.

7. Many of the details from Eugene O'Neill's life in this chapter are from these two books: Louis Sheaffer, *O'Neill: Son and Playwright* (Boston: Little, Brown, 1968), and Stephen A. Black, *Eugene O'Neill: Beyond Mourning and Tragedy* (New Haven: Yale University Press, 1999).

8. Warren Lewis, quoted in Devin Brown, *A Life Observed: A Spiritual Biography of C.S. Lewis* (Grand Rapids: Brazos Press, 2013), 21.

9. C.S. Lewis, *Surprised by Joy* (New York: Harcourt, Brace & World, 1955), 12.

10. Brown, *A Life Observed*, 99-100.

11. David Downing, quoted in Brown, *A Life Observed*, 119.

12. Peter Schakel, *Reading With the Heart: The Way into Narnia* (Grand Rapids: Eerdmans, 1979), 134.

Chapter 8

1. James Bruckner, *The NIV Application Commentary: Jonah, Nahum, Habakkuk, Zephaniah* (Grand Rapids: Zondervan, 2004), 29-30.

2. Ibid., 33.

Chapter 9

1. Ferris Jabr, "How Does a Caterpillar Turn into a Butterfly?," August 10, 2012, *Scientific American, http://www.scientificamerican.com/article/caterpillar-butterfly-metamorphosis-explainer/.* Last accessed October 7, 2015.

2. Molly Webster, "Goo and You," *Black Box.* Radiolab, January 17, 2014, *http://www.radiolab.org/story/goo-and-you/.* Last accessed October 7, 2015.

3. Jabr, "How Does a Caterpillar Turn into a Butterfly?"

4. Molly Webster, "Goo and You."

5. Ibid.

6. Christin Taylor, *Shipwrecked in L.A: Finding Hope and Purpose When Your Dreams Crash* (Indianapolis: Wesleyan Publishing House, 2013), 19.

7. Ibid., 103.

8. Ibid., 110.

9. Ibid., 169.

10. Ibid., 175.

11. Ibid., 179.

Chapter 10

1. *Dirt! The Movie*, a film by Bill Benenson and Gene Rosow (2009, Santa Monica, CA: Common Ground Media, 2009), DVD.

2. Ibid.

3. Ibid.

4. William Bryant Logan, *Dirt: The Ecstatic Skin of the Earth* (New York: Norton, 1995), 40.

5. Frank Coffey and Joseph Layden, *America on Wheels: The First 100 Years: 1896-1996* (Los Angeles: General Publishing Group, 1996), 17.

6. Logan, *Dirt: The Ecstatic Skin of the Earth*, 41.

7. Ibid., 60.

8. Ibid., 60.

9. Kate Murphy, "Killing a Patient to Save His Life," June 9, 2014, *The New York Times. http://www.nytimes.com/2014/06/10/health/a-chilling-medical-trial.html?_r=0.* Last accessed October 8, 2015.

10. Cahleen Shrier, adapted by Tally Flint, "The Science of the Crucifixion," *APU Articles*, March 1, 2002. *http://www.apu.edu/articles/15657/.* Last accessed October 8, 2015.

11. Ibid.

12. Kate Murphy, "Killing a Patient to Save His Life."

13. Ibid.

Chapter 11

1. C.S. Lewis, *The Weight of Glory and Other Addresses* (New York: HarperOne, 2001), 30.

2. Ibid., 30-31.

3. Gilbert Meilaender, *Should We Live Forever? The Ethical Ambiguities of Aging* (Grand Rapids: Eerdmans, 2013), 22-25.

4. Ronald Bailey, "The Methusaleh Manifesto," Reason.com, November 17, 2009, *http://reason.com/archives/2009/11/17/the-methuselah-manifesto*. Last accessed October 8, 2015.

5. Ibid.

6. Ibid.

7. Ibid.

8. C.S. Lewis, *The Weight of Glory and Other Addresses*, 33.

9. Ibid., 42.

ABOUT THE AUTHOR

Joseph Bentz is the author of *Pieces of Heaven: Recognizing the Presence of God* (Beacon Hill Press of Kansas City, 2012) and four other books on Christian living. He is also the author of the fantasy novel *Dreams of Caladria* and three other novels. Bentz is professor of American literature at Azusa Pacific University in Azusa, California. He earned a PhD and MA in American literature from Purdue University and a BA in English from Olivet Nazarene University. He lives with his wife and two children in southern California. More information about his books and speaking is available at his website, josephbentz.com. His blog, "Life of the Mind and Soul," also appears at that site.